What Is a Baptist Association?

To God be
the glory!

Robt. Bennett

What Is a Baptist Association?

Jack Keep

REGULAR BAPTIST PRESS
1300 North Meacham Road
Schaumburg, Illinois 60173-4888

Library of Congress Cataloging-in-Publication Data

Keep, Jack, 1934–
     What is a Baptist association? / Jack Keep.
          p.   cm.
     Includes bibliographies.
     ISBN 0-87227-123-4
     1. Baptist associations.   I. Title.
BX6340.K44   1989   89-32118
262'.06--dc20   CIP

© 1989
Regular Baptist Press
Schaumburg, Illinois 60173-4888

CONTENTS

PREFACE

This little volume is the result of an inquiring mind. From the earliest days of my preparation for the ministry, I have heard many conflicting statements with regard to Baptist associations. These, of course, were usually made with great authority. Many of these claims resulted from what an individual thought was the case, or what he had heard from someone else. I was determined to find the answer to the question, "What is a Baptist association?"

Edward Hiscox's manual for Baptist churches, known by a number of titles, was first published in 1859. Its last and most comprehensive revision was published in 1894. This fine volume is still a reference work for Baptist churches. Hiscox's discussion of associations and conventions, however, deals with these societies as they existed in the latter half of the nineteenth century.

Another volume, published in 1860, is *Fifty Years Among the Baptists* by David Benedict. This most helpful book gives us personal insights into the practices of the Baptists in the first half of the nineteenth century.

But I wanted to explore the origin of Baptist associations in America. I wanted a more authoritative answer to my questions from those who first gathered in these societies. The articles in this book are a summary of my journey among the Baptists of colonial times.

I am indebted to those who have published the writings of men like Isaac Backus and Morgan Edwards, as well as the minutes of the Philadelphia Baptist Association, 1707–1807, and other early associations. The published studies of others who have researched the minutes of state associations and churches in the eighteenth century were of great assistance to me.

The research and writing of these articles were done while I served as state representative of the Pennsylvania Association of Regular Baptist Churches. They were first published in the *Keystone Baptist* paper, of which I was editor. The article, "What Is a Baptist Association?" was later printed as a literature item for the Association.

It is my sincere prayer that the reading of this book will give a greater appreciation for the blessings Baptists enjoy in co-operation and fellowship through associations.

—Jack Keep
Dale City, Virginia

*I*NTRODUCTION

My good friend and colaborer in the gospel ministry, Jack Keep, has researched and written on a needed subject. Even in our Baptist schools as well as our Baptist churches, there is an unfortunate ignorance of Baptist polity and history. Baptists do have a magnificent heritage!

While we do not rely upon tradition itself for authority, we should recognize the traditions of our Baptist forefathers that rest upon Biblical truths (2 Thess. 2:15). Baptists are a unique people! Besides local churches, which are autonomous (self-ruling), there are associations, councils, fellowships, societies and conventions. Yet there is not really a "Baptist denomination." Brother Keep has performed a noble task in tracing the origins of how and why Baptist churches began to serve together.

I heartily recommend this book to pastors, laymen and especially college students preparing for the ministry.

—*L. Duane Brown, Ph.D.*
Parsippany, New Jersey

What Is a Baptist Association?

There is at times no little confusion of thought occasioned by want of a clear understanding as to the true nature and real purpose of associations; and that, too, by ministers themselves, who ought to be able expounders of Baptist polity and usage."[1]

When Edward Hiscox penned these words more than ninety years ago, it was with the intention of correcting some of the existing confusion. However, the events of the years following served to cause even greater confusion with regard to Baptist polity. We hear the term "independent Baptist" used to mean "unaffiliated" rather than its intended meaning "autonomous." Baptist churches are, by definition, autonomous, or independent, bodies. However, Baptist churches have historically, like the apostolic church, seen the value of mutual fellowship and cooperation without surrendering their sovereignty.

Definition of a Baptist Association

Language is intended to be precise, but over a period of time and as a result of many circumstances, words lose their precision. Some words become broader than their earlier meanings, and some words become emotive and therefore fail to communicate their intended meanings. The following three terms are defined for the reader to show that they are not synonymous either in usage or in practice:

Denomination. Are Baptists a denomination? This word has taken on a negative connotation in some cases where it is used to refer to the control or overlordship by a religious organization.

However, the word means "to name" or "the name of a class of things," such as coins of different denomination.

In the religious sense, it refers to the various Protestant sects. D. N. Jackson defines a denomination as,

> A group of churches united by common ties of faith and worship. It is informal, no church can be excluded by vote or decree. In this sense Baptists are a denomination. But an Association is not a Denomination.[2]

Hiscox agrees with this view, saying:

> What is the denomination? It is not an organic entity; it has no corporate existence; it is not an ecclesiastical body; it has neither organization, laws, nor officers, and has no means of expressing approval or dissent. It is a mere conception of the aggregate of all the churches.[3]

The term "denomination" distinguishes a group by giving it a name according to its practices of beliefs. To speak of "nondenominationalism" is contradictory. Those who speak of their fellowship this way have established themselves as the *nondenominational denomination*. Baptists are, indeed, a denomination by virtue of their common beliefs, doctrines and practices.

Convention. A convention is a body of delegates or of individuals. In the case of the Southern Baptist Convention, the organization is a corporation of individuals. Its charter, dating from 1845, states that those named in the charter and their successors are incorporated into "a body politic by the name and style of the Southern Baptist Convention."

The Northern Baptist Convention (now American Baptist Churches in the USA) was formed in 1907 by the merging of eight Baptist societies into one organization. This convention is governed by a general board and officers. It is also a corporate organization. The Northern Baptist Convention was the brainchild of liberals Shailer Mathews, of the University of Chicago, and Spencer Dickerson, and since its inception the majority of its presidents have been liberals.

Dr. Hiscox published the last edition of his *New Directory for Baptist Churches* in 1894, just before the organization of the Northern Baptist Convention, but he described the state convention as a "general association" embracing the fields of all the associations in the state. It did not, at that time, embrace the associations themselves. "The Convention," he said, "is a missionary organization...." The membership of these conventions was composed of persons "appointed by contributing churches, delegates sent by cooperating associations, individuals who make themselves annual or life members by the payments of a specified sum . . . to a large extent, a money qualification is insisted on...."[4]

It will be seen in the following discussion that there is a marked distinction between a convention and an association.

Association. What is a Baptist association? Recognizing that an association is not found in the New Testament, as such, although the underlying elements are Scriptural, we will see that Baptist associations have exhibited some shades of difference. We will begin, therefore, with a working definition: A Baptist association is a voluntary fellowship of churches whose messengers gather in stated meetings for mutual fellowship and counsel, to maintain uniformity in faith and practice among the churches and to cooperate in their broader ministries. An association cannot exercise authority over the churches or bind them in any way by its own actions.

The Composition of a Baptist Association

An association is a fellowship of churches. As such, it is not a society that serves the churches but a fellowship through which the churches serve one another. Some Baptists have stressed that the idea of association is relationship rather than organization. They maintain, therefore, that there is a distinction between the association and the "association meeting," which is an organized meeting of the messengers.[5]

Most Baptist historians agree that there is, indeed, this distinction between the concept, or ideal, of the churches associated and the organized body of messengers that meets for business. The use of the term "association of churches" refers to the relationship of the churches in fellowship and cooperation—not membership—since a Baptist church, being autonomous, cannot be a member of anything outside itself.

An association, or associational meeting for the sake of clarity, is an organized body of pastors and messengers for the transaction of business. These messengers may properly be called *members* of the association. This body has its own constitution and articles of faith and is a self-contained body. During the meetings, sermons are preached, reports are read, prayer meetings are held, and business pertaining to the cooperative work of the churches is acted upon. In the eighteenth and nineteenth centuries, local churches looked to the association for its combined wisdom and experience in answering questions arising in their congregations. In all cases, the response of the association was in an advisory capacity only.

Because Baptist associations through the years have left little of historical record, apart from their minutes, and because the minutes are not always precise in their terminology, there is some ambiguity as to whether the messengers were regarded as delegates. Such a view would indicate church authority given to the messengers to act on behalf of, or as representatives of, their local churches.

As a matter of fact, during the early days of Baptists in England, both the Particular (Calvinistic) and General (Arminian) Baptists employed a messenger who was a minister who traveled among the churches. In 1665, Thomas Collier was chosen by the Western Association of Particular Baptists to serve as "General Superintendent and Messenger to all the associated churches."[6] This usage, however, is an exception to the normally accepted idea that a messenger is an individual elected by the local church for the sole purpose of attending the associational meeting.

John E. Steely has made a study of the role of messengers in Baptist history.[7] He points out that the term "represent" is frequently used in formal documents and in informal discussions to identify the function of the messengers from the churches. In fact, the "plan" adopted by the Danbury (Connecticut) Association in 1790 reads: "With the messengers the churches send letters addressed to the Association; in the letters the names of the messengers are mentioned, and *their authority to act for their churches. . . .*"[8]

Steely says this strong language of delegation is not paralleled in any other minutes or association histories that he has studied. Furthermore, "it is so frequently declared that churches do not delegate authority to their messengers, and so frequently denied that Associations have any ecclesiastical authority, that the Danbury Association's language [is] seen as a quite rare exception."[9]

14

The interchangeable use of "delegate" and "messenger" in early records indicates that the word delegate did not carry the implication of authority. Hiscox uses the term delegate while stating that an association is not a representative body because a church cannot transfer its powers and responsibilities to any man or body of men: "Whatever is done while in session, is of authority only to those who do it; that is, the members—the pastors and delegates."[10]

Messengers have an obligation to the association as members of that body, but they also have an obligation to the churches who sent them as messengers. The church may expect that the messenger will bring back a report on the state of the churches and of the proceedings of the association. While the messenger is not delegated with any authority from his church, it may be assumed that he would think carefully about how his congregation would vote when issues arise and votes must be cast. Therefore, it may be assumed that a messenger "represents" his church in a very loose sense of that term.

Description of a Baptist Association

A Baptist association is a voluntary society. Associations came into existence because of a recognized need for fellowship, counsel and mutual assistance, maintenance of uniformity in faith and practice, and cooperation in promoting the missionary and educational goals of the churches. Although the association is an organization of human origin, it is based on Scriptural concepts of cooperation among churches. In 2 Corinthians 8:1–7, Paul refers to a cooperative action of the churches at Macedonia and Achaia in sending a gift to the needy saints at Jerusalem. In verses 17–19 he declares that the messengers who delivered the gift were "chosen of the churches" to do so. There are many other evidences of cooperation among the apostolic churches, but these are sufficient to show that the idea of association is Biblical.

No church is compelled to enter into fellowship with any other organization. Each church is autonomous, "a compact and knit city in itself."[11] Therefore, its choices of association or fellowship are entirely voluntary. Furthermore, any church may withdraw cooperation at any time and for any reasons which seem sufficient to itself. It does have the obligation to abide by the doctrinal standards mutually agreed upon as long as it is associated.

A Baptist association is an autonomous society. It has no authority over the churches and cannot legislate or bind them in any way by its own actions; the church must independently and voluntarily adopt the resolutions, recommendations or advice for itself.

The first general assembly of Baptists in London took place in 1689. This assembly declaimed all "power to prescribe or impose anything upon the faith or practice of any of the churches of Christ,"[12] and further resolved, "whatever is determined by us in any case shall not be binding upon any church till the consent of that church first be had."[13]

An association may define its own constituency. One writer defines a Baptist association as "a self-determining Baptist interchurch community, created and sustained by the churches affiliated with it. . . ."[14] If a Baptist association is a self-determining community, it follows that it has the right to determine its own constituency.

Dr. Robert T. Ketcham reasoned that if a local church made up of sovereign individuals can determine the requirements for membership in the local church, a sovereign association or convention can do the same. He concluded, "It is evident that a Baptist body can define the limits of its own membership without violating the sovereignty of the local church."[15]

An association, then, can withdraw fellowship from any church that deviates in its doctrine or practice from that of the association. In 1749 Benjamin Griffith presented an essay entitled "Power and Duty of an Association" to the Philadelphia Baptist Association. He said:

> For if the agreement of several distinct churches in sound doctrine and regular practice be the first motive, ground and foundation or basis of their confederation, then it must naturally follow that a defection in doctrine and practice in any church in such confederation, or any party in any such church, is ground sufficient for an Association to withdraw from such a church or party . . . and to exclude such from them in some formal manner. . . .[16]

The association is not obligated to seat any messenger holding unsound doctrine or practice, and should a church in association persist in retaining a pastor who is unsound in doctrine and practice or is a disreputable person, they may withdraw fellowship from that church. The purpose of these actions is to maintain the purity and soundness of the body.

End Notes

[1] Edward T. Hiscox, *The New Directory for Baptist Churches* (Philadelphia: Judson Press, 1959), pp. 330, 331.

[2] D. N. Jackson, *Studies in Baptist Doctrine and History* (Little Rock, AR: Baptist Publications Committee, 1974), p. 71.

[3] Hiscox, p. 370.

[4] Ibid., pp. 339, 340.

[5] Jesse Cobb, *Cobb's Baptist Church Manual*, rev. ed. (Little Rock, AR: Baptist Publications Committee, 1972), pp. 196, 197.

[6] A. C. Underwood, *A History of the English Baptists* (London: Kingsgate Press, 1947), pp. 71, 72, 109, 110.

[7] John E. Steely, "Associational Messengers in Baptist History" in *Baptist History and Heritage*, vol. 17, no. 2 (Nashville: Southern Baptist Historical Society), pp. 3–10, 43. [These materials originally appeared in the April, 1982, issue of *Baptist History and Heritage*, publication of the Historical Commission of the Southern Baptist Convention. Used by permission.]

[8] Steely, pp. 4, 5.

[9] Ibid., p. 5.

[10] Hiscox, p. 335.

[11] From the London Confession of 1644 in William L. Lumpkin's *Baptist Confessions of Faith* (Valley Forge, PA: Judson Press, 1969), p. 168.

[12] John T. Christian, *A History of the Baptists* (Texarkana, TX: Baptist Sunday School Committee, 1922), p. 320.

[13] Ibid.

[14] E. C. Watson, *The Baptist Association* (Nashville: Convention Press, 1975), p. 33.

[15] Robert T. Ketcham, "Can a Baptist Body Define the Requirements of Its Own Membership without Violating the Sovereignty of the Local Church?" (Schaumburg, IL: GARBC Literature Item No. 8).

[16] *Minutes of the Philadelphia Baptist Association, 1707–1807.* (Atlas, MI: Baptist Book Trust, n.d.), p. 61.

Additional References

J. M. Pendleton, *Baptist Church Manual* (Nashville: Broadman Press, 1966).

Robert G. Delnay, *A History of the Baptist Bible Union* (Winston-Salem, NC: Piedmont Bible College Press, 1974).

THE BASES AND BENEFITS OF AN ASSOCIATION

According to Walter Shurden in *Associationalism among Baptists in America, 1707–1814*, Baptists in the nineteenth and twentieth centuries have, on the whole, explained the existence of associations based almost exclusively on pragmatic factors. The emphasis has been on church autonomy, practical aspects such as fellowship and cooperative ventures and minimizing associational authority.[1] This viewpoint has been especially true in the latter half of the twentieth century when many men, too young to have been through the modernist-fundamentalist conflict but having heard many "horror stories," are skeptical of associations. As a state representative for an association, I have frequently heard the question, "What do we get out of being a part of this association?" I always hasten to explain that the association is not a "service organization" to the churches but a medium through which churches can serve one another. Many churches affiliate with Christian school associations and other organizations of an interdenominational nature and pay dues with few questions about the propriety of these things. Yet the same churches voice their fears of voluntary association with like-minded Baptist churches.

Colonial Baptists not only had valid bases for association but also recognized many benefits that could be accrued from it.

The Bases of Association

Probably the most significant factors leading to the rise and development of associations in America were practical. There were other factors, of course, and these are mentioned in the minutes of the associations. Shurden said,

> If an eighteenth century Baptist had been asked upon what basis his denomination justified associations, he likely would have answered with a verse of Scripture, a brief statement about the Baptist concept of the church, and an enumeration of practical benefits accruing from interchurch cooperation.[2]

It will be seen, then, that in addition to the practical aspects, there are Biblical and theological reasons for associationalism. Although they are not found in a systematic order in the documents, we will separate these ideas for clarity.

The Biblical Basis of Associationalism

Baptists are said to be a noncreedal people. In the twentieth century, religious liberals have used this argument to oppose any definitive statement of faith as a basis for fellowship. This is not what is meant by noncreedal. Baptists have never drawn authority for their beliefs or practices from creeds. They have, however, drawn up numerous "confessions" or statements of faith, the points of which are carefully and liberally supported with Scripture references.

The most frequently quoted passage of Scripture given in support of associations—both in colonial America and in England—was Acts 15. It was not claimed that the Jerusalem Council was an association or even a prototype, but that it was an example of the propriety of interchurch cooperation and counsel. Acts 15 is quoted in Benjamin Griffith's *Treatise of Church Discipline*, annexed to the Philadelphia Confession in 1743, as well as in his "Essay on the Power and Duty of an Association."

In an early associational history, Burkett and Read said:

> If Paul, Barnabas and others, therefore were delegated by their brethren of the churches at Antioch to assemble, or associate with the apostles and elders at Jerusalem, how much more will the propriety and necessity of such meetings or assemblies, appear to us who do not enjoy their *abilities* nor possess their *powers*.[3]

Several aspects of the Jerusalem Council were noted as worthy of imitation. One of these aspects was the interrelationship, the care of churches for one another. At Jerusalem, doctrinal issues were discussed, debated and decided. A circular letter was sent out advising the churches of the result of the council. The early Baptists also acknowledged the advisory nature of associations as seen in the Jerusalem meeting. The preface to the circular letter from Jerusalem said, "It seemed good to the Holy Ghost and to us . . ." (Acts 15:28). This advisory-only attitude was necessitated by the autonomy of each local church. Yet the Baptists believed that while the advice of corporate Christian wisdom was not binding on the churches, neither should it be flippantly disregarded.

Other Scripture passages also gave support to the development of associations. James Manning used Christ's prayer for unity as the text for his sermon at the second meeting of the Warren Association in 1768. He saw in this prayer a basis for cooperation among Baptists.

Charles O. Screven preached from Ephesians 4:4–6 at the organization of the Savannah Association. He thought Paul's emphasis on one body, one Spirit and one faith was relevant to the founding of a new association.

The cooperative venture of sending aid to Jerusalem from Macedonia and Achaia (Rom. 15:25–28; 2 Cor. 8:1–5), and especially the selection of the messenger (2 Cor. 8:18, 19), lent support to the conduct of associations. Other Scriptures cited in support of associations were Matthew 23:8, Romans 12:5 and 1 Corinthians 1:10.

It is important to realize that although colonial Baptists (as well as present-day Baptists) saw Biblical justification for associations, they did not claim to be restoring some ancient ecclesiastical organization. Interchurch cooperation is Biblical; an advisory council is Biblical; but any organization having power over a local church is not Biblical.

The Theological Basis of Associationalism

Baptist theologians have pointed out that the greatest contribution of the Baptists to the religious world has been their doctrine of the church. This is a very significant point, for it is here that Baptists differ from other denominational bodies. All of the Baptist distinctives are inextricably bound up in their doctrine of ecclesiology. From a doctrinal perspective, the Baptist concept of the church provides the theological basis for associationalism.

In Britain and in America, both General and Particular Baptists claimed that the church was both local and mystical. They referred to "churches" and "the church." They acknowledged a relationship of believers beyond the local church, although the primary emphasis was on the local body. A local church was autonomous and had the authority under the lordship of Christ to elect officers, determine membership and order worship without interference from without.

Two ideas provided the theological basis for associations. The first was the Baptist idea of the mystical church; the second was the Baptist emphasis on the local church. All who believed the gospel and were regenerate were members of the mystical church. Therefore, all Christians were members of that body and as children of God were related to one another. While all Christians of the Church Age are members of the "church of the firstborn," all living members of the universal church were not received as members in local Baptist churches. Visible, local churches were composed of those who had been converted to Christ and baptized on the profession of their faith. The great Baptist leader, Isaac Backus, began his ministry in a pedobaptist (infant-baptizing) church. In August 1746, some dispute was brought into the church on the subject of baptism. "About three months after," said Backus, "when the heat of controversy was abated, the question was put to my conscience in my retired hours, Where is it, and in what relation to the church, do those stand, who are baptized, but not converted?"[4] He came to see that there was no Scripture that warranted membership for anyone who did not have a "credible profession of saving faith."[5] He then came to the full conviction of the baptism of believers only. For four more years he continued to minister in this church, having both Baptists and pedobaptists in the congregation. He practiced open communion, following Bunyan's argument that "God has received them therefore we ought to receive them."

But the principle of *truth* overweighed this argument, and Backus said that the truth requires baptism *before* the Supper. He reasoned that even the pedobaptists insisted that only those who had been baptized as they esteemed it could attend the Supper. But Baptists were buried in baptism, having confirmed that what was done to them in infancy was not gospel baptism at all. "Therefore, to commune at the Lord's table with any who were only sprinkled in infancy, is parting with truth, by practically saying they are baptized when we do not believe they are."[6]

The issue of open communion arose periodically in the churches and associations, but the response was always that such practice is contrary to the Word of God. The Bethel Association of South Carolina, in response to a query in 1795, declared that it was disorderly to commune with other denominations. The revivals of 1800 and following caused further questions along these lines, due to the intermingling of various denominations in the revival meetings, but the association and the churches maintained their position.[7] The Appomattox Association of Virginia discussed the question in 1805 and firmly settled that "none but persons baptized upon a profession of faith were proper communicants."[8] The question arose in these places because it was recognized that Christians of other persuasions were godly men and women. Semple responded to this argument by saying, "It was certainly a very erroneous mode of forming an opinion. If open communion be wrong in itself, it cannot be made right by the practice of men, however exemplary they may be in other respects."[9] The Philadelphia Association also discussed the issue, arriving at a similar conclusion in 1784.[10]

These doctrinal restrictions placed on membership and communion in local churches provided a sense of spiritual unity among Baptists and established a theological basis for associations of Baptist churches. This oneness was expressed in the practices of local churches of assisting one another in need, of dismissing members from one church to another, in the calling of various kinds of councils and in letters of communication between churches and between associations.

The Practical Basis of Associations

I said in the beginning of this chapter that in this latter half of the twentieth century we usually emphasize the practical value of associations. But practical considerations also brought colonial Baptists together in associations. In 1707 the churches were invited to send messengers to the first meeting of the Philadelphia Baptist Association to discuss things that "were wanting [lacking] in the churches."[11] A reading of the minutes of this and other associations reveals the practical issues that made association desirable.

An obvious advantage in association was fellowship. Some churches were geographically far removed from others, and any opportunity to fellowship with other like-minded Christians was beneficial. An associational meeting provided a time and place for fellowship. In some cases where a congregation was widely scattered, members of that church would fellowship together in a local group, observing communion on a quarterly basis. These local groups eventually became independent churches, but the fellowship among them naturally continued, forming the basis for association.

Another practical consideration was uniformity in doctrine. In our day, Baptist doctrine is under subtle attack. Many Baptist churches have deviated in polity and in practice because of a lack of discernment. They have in practice denied the doctrines that made them distinctively Baptist. The eighteenth-century Baptists discussed these doctrines and debated the issues related to them. Also, fraudulent ministers existed in those days just as they do in ours. The associations identified these men and warned the churches against them.

Churches facing problems that they could not solve themselves would submit queries to the association and receive the advice of the consensus of godly men. This advice, although never obligatory on the churches, was usually accepted. "In the multitude of counsellors there is safety" (Prov. 11:14).

The Baptists were struggling for religious liberty in colonies where other denominations were the established church. Associations became the vanguard for Baptists in this effort. They became a focal point for Baptist unity in defining and articulating their cause.

Baptist associations also provided a medium through which the churches could cooperate in efforts that none could do alone. The training of men for the ministry, printing of literature, planting of new churches, helping weak churches and supporting foreign missions are some of the ways Baptist churches cooperated through associations.

Benefits of Association

Although eighteenth-century Baptists might defend the existence of Baptist associations on a Biblical and theological basis, the organization and continued popularity of these associational gatherings was on a practical level.

For example, the motive of the churches forming the Philadelphia Association was to "consult about such things as were wanting in the church and set them in order."[12]

The Dover (Virginia) Association, in their circular letter of 1794, gave four "indirect advantages" of an association that can be known only by experience. All of these are practical values such as the fellowship of like-minded brethren, the reporting of God's blessing on the churches in other areas, the benefit to the church where the association is held in hearing preachers from other parts and the advantage to those places where the ministers stop on their way to and from the association.[13]

Morgan Edwards considered the usefulness of the Philadelphia Association "so considerable as to recommend such a combination of churches, were there no divine precept or precedent for it."[14] His examples were:

(1) "It hath made the Baptists a respectable body of people in the eye of other societies and of the civil powers on this continent."[15]

Several examples involving religious persecution were given.

(2) "The said combination of churches has in a good measure remedied the pernicious effects of the '*pruritus praedicandi*' which rages so much in America. One of the first resolves is 'That no man shall be allowed to preach among the associated churches except he produce credentials of his being in communion with his church, and of their having called and licensed him to preach.'"[16]

In that day, as in ours, some vain, self-made preachers represented themselves as Baptists, and some immoral or excommunicated men who had brought reproach upon the name Baptist were seeking entrance into the churches.

(3) "The said association has been very beneficial to the churches concerned in many other respects. Some have been supplied with money toward erecting places of worship; some to defend themselves against oppressors, . . . some to relieve their necessities, in difficulties among themselves . . . some with ministerial helps."[17]

(4) "But [what] I deem the chief advantage of this association (and indeed the spring of all the benefits before mentioned) is, that it introduces into the visible church what are called joints and bands whereby the whole body is knit

together and compacted for increase by that which every part supplieth."[18]

As the reader can see, eighteenth-century Baptists would have defended the existence of Baptist associations on a Biblical and theological basis, but the primary reason for their creation and continuance was the practical benefits. And although Biblical precedent and Baptist theology did not require an *organization* called an "association," it did require association in the sense of spiritual relationship and cooperation among like-minded churches.

End Notes

[1] Walter B. Shurden, *Associationalism among Baptists in America, 1707–1814* (New York: Arno Press, Inc., 1980), p. 69.

[2] Ibid., p. 71.

[3] Ibid., p. 75.

[4] Isaac Backus, *Church History of New England, 1620–1804*, rev. ed. (Little Rock, AR: Challenge Press, 1974), p. 8.

[5] Ibid.

[6] Ibid., p. 9.

[7] Leah Townsend, *South Carolina Baptists, 1670–1805* (Baltimore: Genealogical Publishing Co., Inc., 1978), p. 265.

[8] Robert Baylor Semple, *History of the Baptists in Virginia* (Lafayette, TN: Church History Research and Archives, 1976), p. 274.

[9] Ibid.

[10] A. D. Gillette, ed., *Minutes of the Philadelphia Baptist Association from 1707 to 1807* (Minneapolis: James Publishing Co., n.d.), p. 200.

[11] Ibid., p. 4.

[12] Ibid.

[13] Semple, p. 63.

[14] Morgan Edwards, *Materials toward a History of the Baptists*, vol. 1 (Danielsville, GA: Heritage Papers, 1984), p. 61.

[15] Ibid., pp. 61–62.

[16] Ibid.

[17] Ibid.

[18] Ibid.

ASSOCIATION PRACTICES IN THE 18TH CENTURY

The Yearly or Quarterly Meeting

The first organized association of Baptist churches in America was the Philadelphia Baptist Association, formed in 1707. Baptist churches were few in number, and some of the churches had "arms," or smaller congregations of people, living remotely from the mother church. Some of these smaller congregations did not have ministers to lead them. So from the earliest days in that part of the country the churches appointed a general meeting for preaching and observing the ordinances. The first of these meetings was held at Salem, New Jersey, in 1688, when several were baptized and a deacon ordained.

The people who lived in these places where the general meeting was held called it the yearly meeting because it came to them only once a year, but the ministers and others who attended all the meetings called them quarterly meetings, presumably because they met four times in twelve or thirteen months.

These general meetings continued from 1688 until 1707, when an association of messengers was formed at the general meeting in Philadelphia.

The minutes of the Pennepek church give this account:

Before our general meeting, held at Philadelphia, in the seventh month 1707, it was concluded by the several congregations of our judgment, to make choice of some particular brethren, such as they thought most capable in every congregation, and those to meet at the yearly meeting to consult about such things as were wanting in the churches, and to set them in order. . . . It was then agreed that a person that is a stranger, that has neither letter of recommendation, nor is known to be a person gifted, and of a good conversation, shall not be admitted to preach, nor be entertained as a member in any of the baptized congregations in communion with each other.

It was also concluded, that if any difference shall happen between any member and the church he belongs unto, and they cannot agree, that the person so grieved may, at the general meeting, appeal to the brethren of the several congregations, and with such as they shall nominate, to decide the difference; that the church and the person so grieved do fully acquiesce in their determination.[1]

The association was designed to differ from the yearly meetings chiefly in that it was to be a body of delegates or messengers, whereas the yearly meeting had no such character.[2]

Conduct of Associational Meetings

The annual meeting of the association was the most exciting religious event for eighteenth-century Baptists. Hundreds, even thousands, attended these meetings, sometimes creating a problem in caring for so many people. An old pastor remarked, "House room for twenty-five and heart room for a hundred."[3] The people would cheerfully undertake long, slow journeys of as much as one hundred miles because they expected a blessing. Where there was such zeal, it is not surprising that revivals often took place at these gatherings.

The business of the association consisted in preaching, receiving of letters from the churches as to their condition and statistical report, reading of letters from other associations, dealing with queries from churches and the sending of a circular letter to the churches of the association. This circular letter sometimes was in the form of a pastoral address and sometimes consisted of a more lengthy dissertation on a doctrinal theme. Churches were received and dismissed, supplies were appointed for pastorless churches and officers were elected, generally consisting of a moderator, a clerk and a treasurer.

Without question the preaching and singing were outstanding parts of the associational meeting. David Benedict remarked:

The manner of conducting those which I attended while young was more devotional, less formal than now. . . . There was more preaching and exhortation, more freedom for men of less brilliant powers of speaking to take part in devotional exercises, and an entire absence of agents to bespeak the good will of the people in favor of their good objects.[4]

The agents of whom he spoke were representatives of schools, missionary conventions and other Baptist societies that developed in the nineteenth century.

Queries

The "queries" or questions from the churches also created interest in the association. The Baptist movement, having arisen more or less spontaneously in Europe, did not have a long history of tradition and therefore many questions arose with regard to local church discipline, doctrine and practice. Here are some examples of these queries. The Philadelphia Association was asked whether a church may receive a person immersed by a minister of the church of England, provided the person had been baptized on the professions of faith and repentance. The Association responded affirmatively. The Charleston Association responded affirmatively to a query that a woman may speak in her own defense in the church, with the proviso "so as not to use authority over the man." In 1795, an association advised it was disorderly to commune with other denominations. The Appomattox Association dealt with the subject of open communion in 1805, concurring with the judgment of other associations that none but persons baptized on a profession of faith were proper communicants.

Leah Townsend pointed out that,

Queries from the churches covered the whole field of faith and practice. The duties and conduct of ministers proved disturbing. . . . The consistent policy and advice of the association standardized practice in ordination, steadied the conduct of weak ministers, and soon purged its churches of unworthy or hypocritical pastors.[5]

It is important to emphasize that the associations' responses to the queries were always and only of an advisory nature, and this advisory nature is emphatically spelled out in many places in associational minutes and documents. Nevertheless, the churches recognized the wisdom of the combined judgments of godly men. Although the counsel was not binding, it was generally accepted, and the issues of doctrine and practice met with general agreement among Baptist associations.

Some questions were debated and discussed with great earnestness, enlivening interest and increasing attendance at associational meetings.

Walter B. Shurden wrote:

Unity among the churches was promoted as the discussion helped clarify Baptist doctrines and principles. Historically, the queries have importance because they reveal the life situation of early Baptists. A reading of the queries submitted to associations gives appreciable insight into the multiplied problems confronting eighteenth century Baptists.[6]

Circular Letters

Prior to 1774, the Philadelphia Association sent a warm pastoral letter to the churches urging them to continue in unity and in prayer and generally encouraging them in the work and worship of the Lord. In the 1774 meeting, the association decided to send a circular letter dealing with some particular article of faith of their confession. Abel Morgan was appointed to prepare this letter. The plan was as follows:

I. That the contents of the general letter shall consist of observations and improvements of some particular article of faith contained in our confession. . . .

II. The churches were to be cautioned against innovation in doctrine and practice and to watch against and avoid error wherever, and by whomever, they arise.

III. Suitable endeavors should be made to resolve cases and questions proposed by the churches to the best of our knowledge according to the Scripture.

IV. That all seasonable counsel and advice be given to the churches.

V. That records be kept of all the copies of letters sent from and received by the association.[7]

In subsequent years, the circular letter dealt with the articles of the Philadelphia Confession as well as the subjects of the divine origin of the gospel, baptism of the Holy Ghost, foreign missions, the nature of prayer and the qualifications of a gospel minister, to name a few examples.

Other Practices

Some of the practices of the eighteenth-century Baptists differed considerably from those of today. It must be recognized that the eighteenth century was a pioneering era in America, a time of conflict with Britain and a period of development of the Baptist movement in this country. Besides the influence of English, Welsh and Dutch Baptists, there were the "home-grown" Baptist movements in New England in the seventeenth century and the Separate Baptist movement about the time of Whitefield.

The formation of associations and the discussion of queries from the churches helped to clarify and establish consistent Baptist doctrine and practice in the churches. In time, these usages were refined even further. The laying on of hands on baptized believers and the office of ruling elders in some churches, ordinations, baptisms and communion at association meetings largely disappeared by 1800. Eighteenth-century Baptists often used the term "sacrament" for ordinance and "delegate" for messenger without the sharp distinction we make today in these terms.

Laying on of Hands

The practice of laying on of hands evidently originated with Benjamin Keach, who, in a book he wrote in the 1670s in England, urged this practice as a "sacred ordinance." The Welsh Tract Church in New Jersey, after some other doctrinal difficulties, adopted Keach's Baptist confession along with the article on laying on of hands. Earlier, the Welsh Tract Church had refused to enter into a friendly relationship with the Pennepek church in Pennsylvania because Pennepek did not acknowledge laying on of hands. When the Philadelphia Confession was published in 1742, it included Keach's article on laying on of hands as "an ordinace of Christ." Other American associations did not follow suit, however. The Charleston Association omitted this article in all editions, and several Virginia associations omitted the article in 1806, because the practice had fallen into disuse in Virginia by 1780.

The historian Robert Baylor Semple, in writing of the Ketocton Association, said that for twenty years after its organization in 1766 the custom was invariably practiced. But "after the great revival, first the necessity and then the propriety of it began to be questioned until it was finally disused, and in the revisal of the confession of faith, that article was expunged."[8]

While some of the churches of South Carolina observed this
 31

practice, it had almost ceased by 1800. As early as 1744, when the Reverend Isaac Chandler attemped to introduce this practice in the Euhaw, South Carolina, church, it caused such uneasiness that the practice was dropped.

Ruling Elders

The office of ruling elders was never a universal practice among Baptists. Some of the confessions allow for its existence, but its practice was evidently influenced by the religious persecution of dissenters in the mid-1600s and the development of the Westminster Confession. Lumpkin says:

> . . . It was important that dissenters form a united front, which might be demonstrated by a show of doctrinal agreement among themselves. The very document which would be best proof of this agreement on essential matters was at hand, the Westminster Confession.[9]

This confession became the basis of the second London Confession and the Philadelphia Confession. However, as early as 1611, the English Baptists at Amsterdam, in their Declaration of Faith, claimed only two offices, elders and deacons, and further stated, "And there being but one rule for elders, therefore but one sort of elders." Followers of John Smith published a confession in 1612, which stated that "Christ hath set in His outward church two sorts of ministers: viz., some who are called pastors, teachers, or elders, who administer the word and sacraments, and others who are called deacons. . . ."[10]

In the Carolinas a few churches had ruling elders, but the office among them was gradually dropped.

David Benedict believed the practice may have been taken from the Presbyterians (as was evidently the case in England) or taken from the words "the elders that rule well" in 1 Timothy 5:17.

He said, "Ruling elders, in addition to deacons, in former times in a few instances, were found among the Baptists; but at present (1859), I know of no church of our persuasion where this office is maintained."[11]

He stated his belief that in the case of the New Light or Separate Baptists from New England, the practice of ruling elders was a carryover from the Puritans, from whom they had come.

Ruling elders were almost everywhere met with among the Puritans of this country in early times, but we do not find them anywhere among the old Baptists, who came out from them, till we come down to those which arose in the New Light stir. The few churches in which these offices were found were mostly in the middle states.[12]

It appears from the historical evidence that when the office of ruling elder appeared among Baptists, it was due to the influence of other denominational contacts and that the churches eventually restored the Baptist view of two offices—those of pastor/elder/bishop and deacons.

Semple made an interesting observation regarding plurality of pastors in the North Fork (Virginia) church of the Mountain Association. He observed that the pastor had become infirm through age and so Daniel Keith was associated in the pastoral care. Semple said:

> This circumstance often occurs in England, but rarely in Virginia. It much oftener happens in Virginia that one minister is pastor of three or four churches than that the same church has more than one pastor. The committing of the ministerial authority of the church to more than one elder has in this country often been found upon experience to be bad policy. It often creates parties.[13]

Ordinances

Walter Shurden maintains that the strict view that baptism and the Lord's Supper are to be observed only by the local church is due to the Landmarkists in the mid-nineteenth century. He points out that celebration of the Lord's Supper was a common associational practice in the eighteenth century, and he indicates a common belief among Baptists that all Baptist churches were one in Jesus Christ, and that the association expressed that oneness. All three major Baptist groups—General Baptists, Regular Baptists and Separate Baptists—observed the ordinances at interchurch gatherings. "During the period 1707 to 1814, the observance of the Lord's supper was a regular feature of many associations and not a rare, unbaptistic act occasioned by the loss of emphasis on local church autonomy."[14]

While eighteenth-century Baptists may have observed the Lord's Supper at association meetings on the basis of their oneness within the mystical Body of Christ, they did not include believers of other denominations in this practice. In fact they steadfastly maintained this position in every case of inquiry. When the Brush Creek church inquired of the Bethel Association whether it was disorderly to commune with other denominations, the answer was yes. The mingling of the Baptists with other denominations during the Great Revival of 1800 caused some confusion along these lines (as it does today), since the Lord's Table was often observed at these gatherings. The Baptists, however, did not participate in the Lord's Supper. Two churches, Rocky Creek and Bethel, questioned the Bethel Association in 1802 with regard to communing with other denominations, and the emphatic negative on the practice braced the members to maintain their position.

Ordination

The practice of ordination by an association was a rare occurrence, although questions regarding ordination were discussed and debated.

The Dover (Virginia) Association debated a query in 1786, "How is ordination legally performed?" The one side maintained that the laying on of hands by a presbytery of ministers was enough to ordain any man properly recommended. The presbytery would examine his call to the ministry and doctrines while the church would take cognizance of his moral character. The opposition took exception to this, strenuously maintaining that a call from a church was sufficient ordination. The question was held over until 1792.

In the 1792 association, the party that opposed ordination by presbytery (today we refer to it as a council) argued that the independence of the local church was destroyed if it could not obtain the services of a minister unless he had been examined and ordained by a presbytery. They also argued that the churches were better judges of what ministerial abilities suited them; that the laying on of hands in Scripture was with a view to miraculous gifts and, lastly, that such ordination practice gave the local church the appearance of being governed by too many forms.

The other party contended that the New Testament did sanction the laying on of hands where no miraculous consequences resulted; that even though it was a form, it had been used in all ages for setting men apart for the ministry; that no minister or deacon was forced upon a church but by its own consent; that although a church might judge better than a presbytery what suited it, laymen, who had not exercised a public gift, would not be as competent to judge concerning public gifts as a presbytery who had.

After the subject had been investigated for years, the Dover Association finally decided in favor of imposition (laying on) of hands as the custom had been for many years.

The Bethel Association in South Carolina appointed a committee in 1791 to study the matter of ordination. The association had been disturbed by the conduct of some ministers who were guilty of "gross and scandalous crimes."[15] A report in 1792 called for clearest evidences of real piety and ability in candidates and the calling in of three, or at least two, reputable ministers to assist in ordinations. The consistent policy and advice of the Association standardized the practice of ordination and generally improved the quality of ministers in the churches.

In summarizing the matter of ordination in the Carolinas, Townsend said:

If the church decided that he [ordination candidate] had the necessary qualifications, he was usually licensed to preach, and after a year, or even less in some cases, his church, or one desiring to use his services, arranged for his ordination. Though Welsh Neck stated plainly that ordination consisted in the church's choice of a man to office, and needed not the laying on of hands to make it valid, yet a presbytery to examine the qualifications of candidates and to lay hands on them to complete their ordination generally attended.[16]

Benedict remarked:

Councils or presbyteries, as they are termed by our brethren south and west, in former times invariably met in the morning for the examination of the candidates, and in the afternoon for the public services. In the interval a sumptuous dinner was partaken of, either at a public house or at the residence of a wealthy member. This was a wide departure from the custom of primitive times, when they *fasted* and prayed before they engaged in the work of ordination.[17]

An unsusual thing happened in the meeting of the southern district of the Separate Baptist Association of Virginia in 1774. The question arose of whether all the offices mentioned in Ephesians 4:11–13 were still existent in the present-day church. A spirited debate followed, and the association voted to appoint apostles. Three men were appointed whose duties were to see to the work of ordination, to set in order things that were wanting and to make report to the next association.

It is sufficient to inform our readers that this scheme did not succeed. Either the spirit of free government ran too high among the churches to submit to such an officer, or the thing was wrong in itself, and, not being from God, soon fell. . . . In the last decision, it was agreed that the office of apostles, like that of prophets, was the effect of miraculous inspiration and did not belong to ordinary times.[18]

End Notes

[1] Gillette, *Minutes of the Philadelphia Association*, p. 25.

[2] John T. Christian, *A History of the Baptists of the United States* (Texarkana, TX: Bogard Press, 1926), p. 149.

[3] David Benedict, *Fifty Years among the Baptists* (Little Rock, AR: Seminary Publications, 1977), p. 89.

[4] Ibid., p. 87.

[5] Townsend, *South Carolina Baptists*, p. 264.

[6] Shurden, *Associationalism among Baptists*, p. 68.

[7] Gillette, p. 136.

[8] Semple, *Baptists in Virginia*, p. 389.

[9] William L. Lumpkin, *Baptist Confessions of Faith* (Valley Forge, PA: Judson Press, 1980), p. 236.

[10] Ibid., pp. 122, 138.

[11] Benedict, p. 167.

[12] Ibid., pp. 165–167.

[13] Semple, pp. 363–364.

[14] Shurden, p. 94.

[15] Townsend, p. 264.

[16] Ibid., p. 293.

[17] Benedict, p. 105.

[18] Semple, p. 82.

SOCIETIES OF BAPTISTS IN THE 18TH CENTURY

Historians generally claim that the first person in America to advocate Baptist principles was Roger Williams. In 1635, Williams was banished from the Massachusetts Bay Colony for his views respecting individual soul liberty. By 1639, he had become convinced that infant baptism was a perversion of the Biblical ordinance. He then became convinced that without apostolic authority the ordinance should not be practiced at all, and he withdrew from the Baptists. It may be questioned whether Williams was ever truly a thoroughgoing Baptist.

Others claim that there were Baptists among the Pilgrims at Plymouth. Cotton Mather stated that many of the first settlers of Massachusetts were Baptists. Benedict wrote, "As our brethren in the Mother Country had been much intermixed with the dissenting pedobaptists, it is highly probable that the early emigrants of this class continued to do so for the first years of their settlement here."[1] The Baptists were not associated in churches of their own, and when the christening of infants would take place, they would stand with their backs to the minister or walk out in such a manner that everyone understood their statement of protest.

In 1761 Morgan Edwards came from England to pastor the Philadelphia Baptist Church. He resigned in 1771 and became a traveling evangelist for the Philadelphia Baptist Association. It was during these years that he collected his information for an early history of the Baptists in America. Although he published parts of his history, the entire work was never printed. In his notes, Edwards identifies several societies of Baptists in America in his day. In these days when some lament the large number of Baptist groups in our country, we are interested to observe that even when the denomination of Baptists was very small, there were differing societies among them. A survey of these societies, their origin and doctrines gives us a better perspective of the reasons why we have "57 varieties" of Baptists today. Baptists then were associated by doctrinal beliefs, by geographical considerations or both.

Particular Baptists

Morgan Edwards divided the Pennsylvania Baptists into two groups, British Baptists and German Baptists, the latter including "Tunkers" and "Mennonists" who rejected infant baptism. The British Baptists, of whom there were ten congregations, were so universally Calvinist that the terms "particular" and "general" were not used. The Philadelphia Baptist Convention officially adopted the Second London Confession of 1689, with Benjamin and Elias Keach adding two articles to the confession in 1697. These articles involved the singing of hymns and laying on of hands on baptized believers.

In Maryland the Baptists were designated "particular" after the fashion of Baptists in England who embraced the doctrine of particular redemption. These Maryland Baptists also were in association with the Baptists at Philadelphia. In South Carolina, nineteen churches of the Charlestown Association were designated as Particular Baptists. This was the second Baptist association in America, formed in 1751.

In Virginia and North Carolina, Baptists of the "particular" persuasion were designated as "regular" Baptists because they adhered to the Philadelphia Confession of Faith. This term was also applied in order to distinguish them from both Separate Baptists and General Baptists. The Regular Baptists in Virginia formed their own association in 1765, and in North Carolina they formed the Kehukee Association in 1769.

General Baptists

Edwards wrote that the Baptists of Rhode Island were designated "general" Baptists because they held to the doctrine of general redemption and subscribed to the English Arminian Confession of 1660. Lumpkin maintains that the churches of

New England often included both Calvinistic and Arminian Baptists and therefore did not immediately set forth their views in confessions.[2] Other sources support this view, showing that a number of church divisions took place over these doctrines.

Many of the earliest churches in Virginia, Maryland and North and South Carolina were Arminian, and held the views of the English General Baptists, until the Regular and Separate Baptists came among them in the middle of the eighteenth century. Thereafter the General Baptist churches were reconstituted in the Calvinistic position.

Separate Baptists

The Baptists of this order had their roots in the Great Awakening under George Whitefield's preaching. Members of Congregational churches thus converted, and seeking a pure church, were called "New Lights." They separated from the Congregational churches but came to realize that the spiritual church membership they sought could be secured only by the rejection of infant baptism and by practicing the baptism of believers only. Many of these New Lights migrated to the South and multiplied in Virginia and North Carolina.

At first some of the practices of the Separate Baptists were excessive. Morgan Edwards referred to their unusual tones and bodily actions in preaching, "the people crying out and falling down as in fits, and awakening in extacies [sic]; and both ministers and people resemble those in regarding impulses, visions and revelations."[3]

David Benedict referred to their unusual practices such as, "love feasts, laying on of hands, washing feet, anointing the sick, the right hand of fellowship, kiss of charity, and devoting of children or dry christening. They also held to ruling elders, elderesses, deaconesses, and weekly communion.[4]

By the turn of the nineteenth century, most of these practices had disappeared, and the Separates had become much like other Baptists. Edwards wrote that the Separates, like the Regulars, adhered to the doctrines of the Philadelphia Confession.[5] Nor did all the Separates practice the oddities mentioned above.[6]

Keithian Baptists

This group arose from the Quakers in Pennsylvania in 1691

when some, under the leadership of George Keith, denied "the sufficiency of what every man naturally has within himself for the purpose of his own salvation," and consequently magnified the external Word, Christ, and other doctrines above Barclay's measure.[7]

A remarkable incident is referred to by Edwards:

> John Holmes, Esq. (the only Baptist Magistrate in Philadelphia at the time referred to) refused to act with the Quaker Magistrates against the Keithians, alledging [sic] 'That it was a religious dispute and therefore not fit for a Civil Court.' Nay he openly blamed the Court (held at Philadelphia, Dec. 6–12, 1692) for refusing to admit the exceptions which the prisoners made to their jury.[8]

The incident is remarkable because the Quakers, who eschew persecution, were persecuting a dissenter from their own ranks.

These dissenters embraced believer's baptism and became known as Keithian Baptists or Quaker Baptists. In time a dispute among them arose over the Sabbath, which eventually led to the demise of the Keithians. Their head, George Keith, had gone over to the Episcopalians. Some of the group went to the Baptists, some returned to the Penn Quakers and the remainder were transformed into Seventh-Day Baptists.

Seventh-Day Baptists

This group remains to this day although it is a very small group. In the mid-eighteenth century they were found in Pennsylvania, New Jersey and South Carolina. Their distinctive is that of worship on the seventh day, or as Newman put it, "they spend their strength in contending that the substitution of the Lord's Day for the Jewish Sabbath is a heathen perversion that involves a plain violation of a command of God meant to be a perpetual obligation. Their type of thought is distinctly Judaizing."[9]

Rogerene Baptists

This group was found in 1674 in New London, Connecticut, when John Rogers and several members of his family were baptized. John, the most forward of the Rogers brothers, formed his family and others into a church, made a creed and established rules of discipline. The first act of discipline was to excommunicate his brother Jonathan for using medicine. While orthodox in many of their doctrines, this group was very peculiar in others, such as regarding all days of the week the same since the death of Christ. The first day of the week, the Lord's Day, they regarded as the "New England idol" and set about to demolish it by taking work into the meeting house, the women knitting and the men whittling and now and then contradicting the preacher. Other peculiarities of the Rogerenes were nonuse of medicine or doctors, no grace at meals and all prayers to be mental, not spoken.

One large family of Rogerenes named Colver, numbering twenty-one persons, decided to move to New Jersey in 1734. There they became known as Colverites.

It is remarkable that this branch of Rogerenes continued in New Jersey for fifty-six years (at the time of Morgan Edwards's writing) when one considers their contrary nature. In Basking Ridge they were fined and received corporal punishment for disturbing a Presbyterian congregation, but in other places they were carried out of the meeting house with great jesting and confined in stables and barns and once in a hogpen until the worship was over.

It is even more remarkable that the society of Rogerenes lasted for 116 years from its beginning. This is longer than most current Baptist groups have been in existence. At the time of this publication, the Southern Baptist Convention has been in existence for 144 years, the American Baptists for 82 years, the GARBC for 57 years, the Conservative Baptists (as a separate fellowship) for 42 years and the Baptist Bible Fellowship for 39 years.

"It is surprising," said Edwards, "how principles, or education or custom, or something will make people differ from others so greatly, that it is hard to think they are of the same common nature, or are of the same common Maker."[10]

End Notes

[1] David Benedict, *A General History of the Baptist Denomination in America*, quoted in Christian's *A History of the Baptists*, p. 24.

[2] Lumpkin, *Confessions of Faith*, p. 347.

[3] Edwards, *Materials toward a History*, vol. 2, p. 90.

[4] Benedict, *Fifty Years*, p. 164.

[5] Edwards, p. 43.

[6] Ibid., p. 90.

[7] Robert Barclay, the chief apologist for Quakerism, wrote *An Apology for the True Christian Divinity* in 1678. This became the standard theological work of the Quakers. In it he describes the Quaker movement as a religion of the inner light; that is, that every man has naturally within himself sufficient light for his own salvation. Barclay's measure of the Scriptures is that they are a secondary rule and declaration of the truth but not the truth itself. The Keithians denied that the inner light was more sure than the Scriptures.

[8] Ibid., vol. 1, p. 27.

[9] A. H. Newman, *A Manual of Church History*, vol. 11 (Philadelphia: American Baptist Publishing Society, 1903), p. 703.

[10] Edwards, vol. 1, p. 144.

BAPTIST ASSOCIATIONS AND RELIGIOUS LIBERTY

The story of the persecution of the Baptists in America is real. The chronicle of their efforts to secure liberty of conscience for all men would require a good-sized volume.

Although they were not alone as dissenters in this struggle for religious liberty, it is universally agreed that the Baptists were in the forefront of the effort.

The most common approach in presenting the Baptist contribution to religious liberty is to focus on the efforts of individuals such as Roger Williams, John Clarke, Isaac Backus and John Leland. The importance of the labors of these men cannot be minimized, but there is more to the story. As Robert Shurden has pointed out: This biographical approach is severely limited. Especially is this the case with Backus and Leland, whose ministries covered the crucial period in the struggle for religious freedom from 1770 to 1833.

The temptation in Baptist historiography has been to isolate the accomplishments of salient individuals without recognizing and giving due credit to the denominational context within which the individual worked. For eighteenth- and early nineteenth-century champions of religious liberty, this context was the Baptist Association.[1]

Isaac Backus was, in fact, the *agent* of the Warren Association in Rhode Island; and John Leland, along with many other individuals, worked in conjunction with Baptist associations in both Virginia and New England.

Virginia and Massachusetts were the geographical centers of the most militant opposition to the oppression and persecution of the Baptists and other dissenters. I will, therefore, focus on these regions and the contribution of the Baptist associations in these regions in securing religious liberty.

The Virginia Baptists

The Baptists of Virginia came in three groups. The first were emigrants from England who came in 1714 and formed a General Baptist church. They settled in the southeastern part of the state.

The second group came from Maryland in about 1743 and settled in the northwestern section. This group formed a Regular Baptist church in 1751, being in fellowship with the Philadelphia Baptist Association.

A third party, the Separates (already mentioned on pp. 31, 39), came from New England. This group was also known as the New Lights. They were revived by the preaching of George Whitefield, opposed by many of the established clergy in New England and so withdrew from the Congregationalists to form a society of their own. Shubal Stearns, a product of the Whitefield revival, joined the Separates in 1745 and became convinced of believer's baptism in 1751. Migrating to North Carolina in 1755, he and his followers organized a Baptist church there by the name of Sandy Creek. This group became known as the Separate Baptists, and from them came the first Separate Baptist church in Virginia, organized in August 1760.

As Baptists began to grow and multiply in Virginia, supporters of the Church of England, which was the establishment there, began to oppose and then persecute them.

The struggle for religious liberty in Virginia can be divided into three periods. The first period was before 1771, the year that marks the organization of the General Association of Separate Baptists. The second period encompasses the years 1771 to 1783. For these twelve years the General Association of Separate Baptists represented Virginia Baptists as the voice for freedom. The last period, 1784 to 1799, delineates the era when an organization called the General Committee coordinated the efforts of Baptist associations to secure liberty.

We will now discuss these periods in detail.

Before 1771

The Baptists in Virginia at this time were too weak in number to effectively oppose religious inequality. "But an equally important reason," says Shurden, "was the absence of a denominational organization [association] which could stimulate and correlate efforts for religious freedom."[2]

The only existing association before 1771 was the Ketocton Association of Regular Baptists who, with few exceptions, never became as vigorously involved in the struggle for religious liberty as the Separates. While the Regulars were deprived of their liberties and suffered persecution, they did not suffer as much as the Separates. Robert B. Semple gives the reasons:

> The reason why the Regular Baptists were not as much persecuted as the Separates was that they had at an early date applied to the General Court and obtained licenses for particular places, under the toleration law of England. . . . One other reason for their moderate persecution, perhaps, was that the Regulars were not thought so enthusiastic as the Separates; and having Mr. Thomas, a learned man, in their society, they appeared much more respectable in the eyes of the enemies of the truth.[3]

It is believed by historians that no law in existence in Virginia authorized the imprisonment of any person for preaching. The law for preservation of peace, however, was interpreted in this way and used to imprison Baptist preachers.

Evidently the first case of imprisonment for such a crime in Virginia was that of John Waller, Lewis Craig and James Childs in Spotsylvania County in June 1768. They were arraigned as disturbers of the peace. At their trials they were vehemently accused by a certain lawyer who said, "May it please your worships, these men are great disturbers of the peace; they cannot meet a man upon the road, but they must ram a text of Scripture down his throat."[4] After Mr. Waller's defense, the court officials were in confusion and offered to release the men if they would promise not to preach again in the county for a year and a day. They, of course, refused and were sent to jail where they spent the next forty-three days. While in prison, they preached to crowds through the grates. The efforts to stop them could not stifle the enthusiasm of those who came to hear.

Imprisonments and beatings occurred in other places as well, but the persecutors found that imprisonment of preachers tended to the furtherance of the gospel. Baptists meeting together were harassed, baptisms were broken up and the case of any Baptist's failing was greatly exaggerated.

The Church of England was the established church of Virginia and the residents were taxed for the purpose of glebes (parish lands purchased with taxes) and for the salaries of the ministers. In addition, only marriages performed by the clergy of the established church were considered valid. In some cases, licenses were granted for dissenters to preach in certain places, although most of the Baptists did not think it right to obtain such a license.

Virginia Baptists sent their first petition requesting greater religious toleration to the colonial legislature of Virginia in 1770. Part of the appeal was rejected and the remainder ignored. Other protests and petitions met a similar fate.

1771—1783. The General Association of Separate Baptists

The Baptists in Virginia increased in number and in favor with those who were willing to take a closer look. The General Association of Separate Baptists was organized in 1771.

Robert Semple explains further:

So favorable did their prospects appear that toward the close of the year 1774 they began to entertain serious hopes, not only of obtaining liberty of conscience, but of actually overturning the Church Establishment, from whence all their oppression had arisen. Petitions for this purpose were accordingly drawn and circulated with great industry. Vast numbers readily and eagerly subscribed to them. The great success and rapid increase of the Baptists in Virginia must be ascribed primarily to the power of God working among them.[5]

The first action taken by a Separate Baptist association was at the 1774 meeting of the southern district of the association. Letters from several Baptist ministers then in jail were received at this association. David Tinsley, for example, had at that time been in the Chesterfield jail for a period of four months and sixteen days. He preached to crowds through the grated windows, and some came away weeping and others rejoicing and many were converted to Christ. The association agreed to raise contributions for the aid of Tinsley and the others. The following resolution was entered into:

Agreed to set apart the second and third Saturdays in June as public fast days, in behalf of our poor blind persecutors, and for the releasement of our brethren.[6]

Shurden says, "Separate Baptists soon recognized that the exigencies of their time required more than fasting and praying. Organized and persistent protests were needed."[7]

By 1775, the northern and southern districts of the General Association, which had divided in 1773, were meeting as one again. The great object at this time was to strive together for the abolition of church establishment in Virginia.

On March 17, 1774, an amended bill on the issue of toleration was presented in the House of Burgesses. This bill was not acceptable to the Baptists, who protested that, "Not admitting public Worship, except in day time is inconsistent with the laws of England, as well as the practice and useage [sic] of the Primitive Churches and even of the English Church itself."[8] The bill did not become law. The Revolution was on, and the Baptists now attacked established religion itself and eventually won the victory for liberty of conscience.

At the 1775 association, the messengers resolved to circulate petitions throughout the state to obtain signatures to be sent to the Virginia General Assembly. The essence of these petitions was "that the church establishment should be abolished, and religion left to stand on its own merits, and that all religious societies should be protected in the peaceable religious principles and modes of worship."[9] They also petitioned the assembly for permission to preach to the army.

Jeremiah Walker, John Williams and George Roberts were appointed to take the petitions to the legislature. The first-mentioned petition was circulated and signed by ten thousand dissenters of various denominations throughout the state. Baptists wanted more than toleration—they wanted full religious liberty. Annually the General Association, until it was divided into four associations, appointed committees to remonstrate before the Virginia legislature regarding religious equality. Among the issues addressed was the general assessment for the support of the clergy. In 1779 the law enforcing the established church was repealed, and the tax for the support of the clergy was suspended.

In the 1780 association, a letter was received from a committee of Regular Baptists requesting that the association appoint a similar committee to consider national grievances in conjunction. This overture, and other circumstances leading to the formation of the General Committee in 1783, eventually led also to the union of the Separates and Regular Baptists in Virginia.

1784—1799. The General Committee

The large number of churches and the great distances traveled by messengers rendered the General Association impractical. The glue that had held the association together was the apprehension arising from civil oppression. It was agreed to divide into four separate associations and to form a General Committee composed of not more than four delegates from each association to meet annually "to consider matters that may be good for the whole society."[10] The Philadelphia Confession of Faith was adopted with an explanation that no person was bound by every point in the confession.

One of the points governing this committee follows:

> The Committee thus composed shall consider all the *political grievances* of the whole Baptist Society in Virginia, and all references from the District Associations respecting matters which concern the Baptist Society at large.[11]

The committee began its work and decided that among the political grievances of the Baptists were the law for the solemnization of marriages, the vestry law[12] and the incorporation of religious societies. The law regarding marriages restricted licenses by the county courts to not more than four dissenting ministers within each sect; it also restricted celebration of the rite to within the limits of their counties.

In the meeting of 1784, a memorial requesting repeal of the vestry law and alteration of the marriage law was sent in the hands of the Reverend Reuben Ford to be presented at the next assembly.

It is of considerable interest to us, in a day when it is thought by many that separation of church and state means passively suffering the violation of our liberty, that the *eighteenth-century Baptists were anything but passive*. Annually they sent their representatives to the assembly with memorials, petitions and grievances. The men who were appointed by the associations were designated as "agents" of the association, or of the General Committee. Today, these men would probably be called lobbyists. The associations were extremely aggressive in the pursuit of religious liberty, and we are the beneficiaries of their efforts.

In the General Committee meeting August 1785, Reuben Ford reported that, as a result of the petition, certain amendments to the marriage law were made that were favorable. He also reported that a bill had almost been passed into law that would levy a general assessment for teachers of the Christian religion. The Baptists passed a resolution against it and urged each county to prepare a petition against it to be presented to the General Assembly. They further appointed Reuben Ford as a delegate to wait on the General Assembly with a remonstrance and petition against such assessment.

In the meeting of 1786, Reuben Ford reported that the assessment bill did not pass, but, on the contrary, an act passed explaining the nature of religious liberty. This act was authorized by Thomas Jefferson and reads:

Be it enacted by the General Assembly, that no man shall be compelled to frequent or support any religious worship, place or ministry whatsoever; nor shall be enforced, restrained, molested or burthened in his body or goods, nor shall otherwise suffer on account of his religious opinions or beliefs; but that all men shall be free to profess and by argument to maintain their opinions in matters of religion, and that the same shall in no wise diminish, enlarge or affect their civil capacities. enacted December 16, 1785[13]

The General Assessment Bill would have collected taxes, the benefits of which would have been paid to the ministers of all denominations. Many of the former dissenting churches supported this bill. Some experienced disagreement between the ministry and the laity. But it was the Baptists alone who remonstrated against the measure and won the day with the help of men like James Madison and Thomas Jefferson.

The business of 1787 included a report by Reuben Ford and John Leland, who had presented a memorial requesting repeal of the act incorporating the Protestant Episcopal Church as a religious society. The whole issue of incorporation and its implications is discussed by Semple in view of a suit in Virginia in 1802.[14] Baptists have generally accepted the practice, but in view of present bureaucratic incursions into religious liberties, perhaps the subject should be restudied.

At this meeting of 1787, the Separates and Regular Baptists found common ground for fellowship. The terms *Regular* and *Separate* were dropped and the name United Baptist Churches of Christ in Virginia was adopted.

The next meeting of the General Committee was in March 1778. At this session a major topic was whether the proposed Federal Constitution made sufficient provision for the secure enjoyment of religious liberty. It was the unanimous opinion of the committee that it did not.

It was also determined that petitions should be presented to the next General Assembly asking for the sale of the vacant glebes as public property. This memorial and similar petitions were presented from this committee every year until 1799 when they gained their object.

In August 1788, the committee met again at which time they wrote a letter congratulating Washington on his elevation to the presidency and declaring their concern for the rights of conscience under the Constitution recently adopted. Washington sent a gracious reply, assuring them of his support of religious liberty (see Appendix 6, p. 83).

Following the meeting of 1789, a number of other subjects not relating to religious liberty were taken up so that some associations and individuals expressed concern that the General Committee was exercising too much power. This and other causes led to the decline and dissolution of the General Committee. Their last act was to recommend to the associations a General Meeting of Correspondence to promote and preserve union and harmony among the churches.

The General Committee served an important place in achieving the goal of religious liberty, not only for the people of Virginia, but for the entire new nation.

The New England Baptists
Early History

The first Baptists in America were located in New England. This area was settled by Separatists, or Pilgrims, who came to Plymouth in 1620. The Puritans came to Massachusetts Bay in 1628. The Separatists were North of England men who denounced the Church of England, fled to Holland and finally came to the New World. The Puritans did not break with the

Church of England but dissented from some of its practices and, because of persecution, came to the New World. The Separatists were described as men with "hearts full of charity, kindness and toleration, their minds broadened by experience in a land where religion was free to all men."[15] The Puritans were quite the opposite—they desired liberty for themselves but were not willing to grant liberty to others.[16]

John Christian states that although there is "no certainty that any of the Pilgrim Fathers were Baptists . . . there was from the first a Baptist taint about Plymouth."[17]

Cotton Mather stated that "many of the first settlers of Massachusetts were Baptists and that they were as holy and faithful and heavenly people as any, perhaps in the world."[18]

David Benedict added, "As our brethren in the Mother Country had been much intermixed with the dissenting pedo-baptists, it is highly probable that the early emigrants of this class in the infant colony, continued to do so for their first years of settlement here."[19]

The first organization of Baptists took place in Rhode Island sometime before 1639, but there had been preaching and church services at least two years before that time.

Roger Williams, banished from the Massachusetts Bay Colony for his views on religious liberty and separation of church and state, came to Rhode Island where he was encouraged by a Mrs. Scott, a Baptist, to make an open profession. Williams was then baptized by a man named Holyman who he in turn baptized along with ten others. Four months later he left the little congregation because he had doubts about the validity of his baptism.

"For him," said Dr. S. L. Caldwell, "there was no church and no ministry left. The apostolic succession had ceased. It was the baptizer, not the baptism, about which he doubted. . . . He went out of the church, left the little congregation behind, preached when and where he could, and became a 'seeker' the rest of his days. And during the rest of his days he never came to a 'satisfying discovery' of a true church or ministry."[20]

John Clarke, a Baptist minister before he left England, came to Newport, Rhode Island, in March 1638. According to the inscription on his tombstone and other records, he began conducting services at that time and gathered a church shortly thereafter. In 1663 he obtained, from Charles II, a charter that secured to the people of Rhode Island "free and full enjoyment of judgment and conscience in matters of religion."[21]

In 1651, Clarke, Obadiah Holmes and John Crandal were arrested in Lynn, Massachusetts, for preaching and observing Baptist worship. All three were fined and jailed, and Holmes was severely beaten with thirty lashes from a three-tailed whip. In 1659, two Quaker men were hanged at Boston; in 1661 a woman and a man were hanged. The Baptists in Boston built a house for worship in 1679, but the following year a law was passed to take it away from them if they continued to meet in it.

A royal charter was granted to Massachusetts in 1691 in which liberty of conscience was afforded to all except Roman Catholics. However, for a long time thereafter, Congregational churches enjoyed preferential treatment by the civil authorities. The religious rights of dissenters were restricted. Baptists and other dissenters were forced to pay taxes for the support of Congregational ministers. In some cases, their goods or lands were seized and sold for payment of the tax. Isaac Backus wrote;

When the new Charter arrived, May 14, 1692, the Country was so involved in confusion about witchcraft, that twenty persons were executed on that account in about four months. And when their general court met, on October 12, they made laws to compel every town to have and support an orthodox minister and to empower their courts to punish every town who neglected it. The whole power of choosing and supporting religious ministers was put into the hands of the voters in each town. . . . Formerly the Church had governed the world, but now the world was to govern the Church.[22]

Between the years 1727 and 1733, twenty-eight Baptists, two Quakers and two Episcopalians were imprisoned in Bristol, Massachusetts, for the ministerial tax. In 1751 a pastor, deacon and church members were imprisoned in Sturbridge. The pastor was banished as "a vagrant and vagabond,"[23] and the church property was confiscated and sold to pay the ministerial tax.

The provincial law of 1770 exempted the Baptists from the tax, providing they gave certificates to the town assessor, signed by their ministers and three other Baptists, that they regularly and conscientiously attended Baptist worship. This law did little to relieve those who lived far from a meeting house, or those who were infirm. Nor did it protect from local tyranny and intolerance. Some of the more conscientious refused to fill out the exemption certificates because to do so would acknowledge the authority of civil government to rule in the affairs of religion.

The Constitution of 1780 did not improve the position of the Baptists. Christian wrote,

> In reality the article on religion was reactionary. It not only continued the religious system of the province but exalted it to a fundamental law, out of reach of ordinary legislative enactment. The provincial system, which was still in force in 1780 may be described as compulsory support of at least one Congregational Church in each town....[24]

The Warren Association

The most important development in securing liberty of conscience in New England was the organization of the Warren Association, in Rhode Island, in 1767. This association was not the first in New England to appeal to civil authority for religious equality. In 1729 an association of General Baptists had appealed to the General Assembly in Connecticut to exempt Baptists from paying taxes to any but their own ministers. The Warren Association, however, became the standard-bearer in the struggle against the religious establishment. The minutes of the association in 1769 stated: "Many of the letters from the churches mentioned grievous oppressions and persecutions from the 'Standing Order,' especially the Church at Ashfield where religious tyranny had been carried out to great lengths."[25]

As a result of these reports, the association appointed two committees. One committee was responsible for preparing petitions to be sent to the General Courts of Massachusetts and Connecticut. The other committee was to present the requests to the courts. In 1769, the association adopted a "plan to collect grievances" that included the following intention: "This is to inform all the oppressed Baptists in New England, that the Association of Warren ... is determined to seek remedy for their brethren, where a speedy and effectual one may be had...."[26]

Each year from 1769 until 1805, the association appointed a Grievances Committee that was to discover these incidents of persecution and seek legal redress.

In addition to the Grievances Committee, an "agent" for the association was appointed. Hezekiah Smith was the first agent chosen to travel to England and, along with two prominent English ministers, to request the assistance of the king in relieving persecution in New England. Although Smith never made the trip, one of the English ministers carried the appeal to the king and help was obtained. John Doves was the second agent chosen, but he died before making any significant contribution. Isaac Backus then became the agent of the Warren Association in 1772. He is remembered as the most vigorous champion of religious liberty and separation of church and state in the history of the American Baptists. Had he not been chosen as agent for the Warren Association, he might never have become the great spokesman he was for religious liberty. Most of his articles and messages on religious freedom were written after he became agent. His petitions, memorials and remonstrances were signed, "Agent for the Baptist Churches." His expenses were paid by the association, and his strategy for achieving separation of church and state was forged in conjunction with the Grievances Committee of the Warren Association.

"In a real sense," says Shurden, "the Warren Association helped Isaac Backus become a famous fighter for religious freedom. Certainly, Backus cannot be adequately evaluated apart from the Association."[27]

When the Continental Congress met in Philadelphia in 1774, the Warren Association sent Backus to cooperate with the Philadelphia Association in appealing to the Congress to assist in obtaining religious liberty. Backus wrote:

And when they [the Warren Association] met at Medfield, September 13, 1774, they chose an agent [Backus] to go to Philadelphia, when the first Congress was sitting there, to join with the Philadelphia Association, to endeavor to secure our religious rights, while we united with our Country in the defense of all our privileges. And when he came there, said Association elected a large committee to help in the affair; and they obtained a meeting of the four delegates from Massachusetts, before other members of Congress, in the evening of October 14; to whom a memorial of our grievances about religious matters was read. This, two of these delegates endeavored to answer, and denied that we had any reason to complain on those accounts. But when leave was given for a reply, plain facts silenced that plea.[28]

Religious Liberty Gained

The Baptists' support of the War for Independence won them respect throughout the colonies. They had the most to gain and the least to lose with the exception of the Baptists of

Rhode Island who, nonetheless, gave full support to the cause. The Baptist influence in securing the adoption of the Constitution and the Bill of Rights has been well documented in many sources.

Massachusetts retained an established church in Congregationalism until 1833. After the turn of the century, however, the Baptists and other dissenters enjoyed considerable freedom, although there were isolated cases where Baptists were taxed for support of Congregational churches. The Warren Association, after 1805, gave a lesser amount of attention to these matters.

It cannot be denied that Baptist associations in the eighteenth century were exceedingly aggressive in opposing those laws that infringed on complete liberty of conscience. The agents they sent before the assemblies opposed such things as licenses for churches or preachers. They also opposed governmental "exemptions" from taxes for support of the ministry—not because they did not want exemption but because they denied that civil government had any right to collect such taxes. The Baptist of today who thinks separation of church and state means passive submission to civil intrusion in the affairs of the church would be very much out of place among the early Baptists of America!

In 1811, the writer of the Warren Association's circular letter penned, "We meet under external circumstances far different from our fathers. Unmolested in the enjoyment of our religious privileges, we sit quietly under our vine and under our fig-tree."[29]

Now as we approach the two hundredth year of religious liberty in America, we must say, "Woe to them that are at ease in Zion" (Amos 6:1)!

End Notes

[1] Shurden, *Associationalism among Baptists*, p. 202.

[2] Ibid., p. 203. ["Denominationalism" is used in the sense of "a body having common beliefs, doctrines and practices." See Chapter 1, "What Is a Baptist Association?"]

[3] Semple, *Baptists in Virginia*, p. 383.

[4] Ibid., p. 30.

[5] Ibid., p. 43.

[6] Ibid., p. 78.

[7] Shurden, p. 205.

[8] Christian, *History of the Baptists*, p. 260.

[9] Semple, p. 85.

[10] Ibid., 92.

[11] Ibid., 95.

[12] The vestry was a body of men elected by the people in each parish to govern the affairs of the established church, which was the Church of England. The vestry law required all ministers to be conformable to the doctrine and discipline of the Church of England. It also excluded dissenters from being eligible to serve on the vestry, thus denying them their civil rights. Moreover, dissenters were compelled to pay taxes for the support of the established church and its clergy.

[13] Ibid., p. 509.

[14] Ibid., p. 253.

[15] Christian, p. 19.

[16] Ibid.

[17] Ibid., p. 24.

[18] Quoted in Christian, p. 24.

[19] Ibid.

[20] Ibid., p. 38.

[21] S. Adler and J. R. Graves, eds., *The First Baptist Church in America* (Texarkana, TX: Baptist Sunday School Committee, 1939), p. 13.

[22] Backus, *Church History of New England*, pp. 94–95.

[23] Christian, p. 84.

[24] Ibid., p. 86.

[25] Quoted in Shurden, p. 211.

[26] Quoted in Shurden, "Warren Minutes," p. 213.

[27] Shurden, p. 215.

[28] Backus, p. 140.

[29] Shurden, p. 215.

BAPTIST ASSOCIATIONS AND MISSIONS

Historically Baptist people have been missions-minded people. While sometimes associated according to differing doctrinal views such as General and Particular Baptists, they have reproduced after their kind and have established churches. This is evident by the growth of the Baptist movement in both Europe and America in the seventeenth and eighteenth centuries.

In America, origins have sometimes been the determining factor in forming distinctive Baptist bodies. The General and Particular Baptists came from the British Isles. After establishing churches here, they formed their own associations. The Separate Baptists, whose roots were in congregationalism during the Great Awakening, also formed their own associations.

These and other Baptist bodies spread the gospel and established churches at home, and in time some were united in the foreign missions enterprise in the early nineteenth century.

Earliest Mission Endeavors

The eighth chapter of Acts tells of a great persecution against the church at Jerusalem. The believers were scattered throughout Judaea and Samaria. As a result, the gospel was proclaimed, as "they that were scattered abroad went every where preaching the word" (Acts 8:4).

The thirteenth chapter of Acts opened a new phase of gospel endeavor as Paul and Barnabas were sent from the local church at Antioch to the work for which the Holy Spirit had called them. The method these first missionaries employed was the planting of churches in the cities they visited.

The two means that have most frequently resulted in the organization of Baptist churches throughout history are the migration of believers and the sending of missionaries. Baptists generally agree on two principles set forth in Acts 13: (1) The local church is the sending agency for missions; and (2) missionary work results in the organization of local churches.

Baptist Associations and Missions

"Though Baptists did not form Associations for missionary purposes," writes Alan Neely, "an evangelistic and missionary impulse was clearly discernible well before the seventeenth century. Associations in the British Isles and North America were engaged in various kinds of missionary activities several decades prior to the formation of the Baptist Missionary Society [1792]."[1]

Seventeenth-century Particular Baptist (Calvinistic) Associations in England, Wales and Ireland not only encouraged "gifted brethren" to minister as missionaries to weaker congregations but provided them with financial aid. In addition, queries from the congregations to the association frequently dealt with missionary matters.

The Philadelphia Baptist Association, formed in 1707, was soon involved in the ministry of evangelism and missions. By 1755 this association was providing support for missionaries on evangelistic tours. In 1766 the association established a special fund to provide itinerant evangelists for destitute churches. Morgan Edwards, who served ten years as pastor of Philadelphia's First Baptist Church, was chosen as evangelist-at-large for the association in 1771. He was followed by John Gano, who later served as a chaplain and was a heroic soldier in the Continental Army and then became pastor of the First Baptist Church of New York City. Gano was outstanding in his work as an itinerant missionary throughout the South.

Missionaries working under the Philadelphia Baptist Association helped plant churches from New England to South Carolina as well as Canada. As the churches multiplied, new associations were formed, which in turn carried on missionary endeavor. From 1751 to 1787, fourteen new associations were formed. This zeal explains why the Baptists in America grew from twenty churches in 1700 to more than two thousand churches a century later.

Henry C. Vedder claimed that the secret of the Baptists' phenomenal growth after 1800 was the Baptist associations, many of which were de facto mission agencies, "existing chiefly for the purpose of encouraging the weaker churches and establishing of new churches in promising localities."[2]

The Sandy Creek Association in North Carolina was organized in 1758, the second Baptist association in the South. For twelve years this association consisted of messengers from Separate Baptist churches in North Carolina, South Carolina and Virginia. Its annual meetings were, without question, for evangelistic and missionary purposes. Large numbers of people came great distances to join in the singing and to hear the preaching. Many of these, having only heard of the Baptists, requested that a Baptist preacher be sent to their area.

The business sessions of the association dealt mainly with a response to these requests. Someone from the association would be designated to go to these places and preach the gospel. The result of these labors was that in seventeen years the Sandy Creek Association became "mother, grandmother, and great-grandmother to 42 churches from which sprang 125 ministers."[3]

In the North, the Shaftsbury Association, formed in 1781 of churches in Vermont, Massachusetts and New York, also developed a missionary program. They appointed a committee to receive and administer missionary monies, approve missionaries, recommend their tenure and areas of work and manage their financial support. Until 1802, the missionary enterprise was an integral part of the association.

The Founding of Mission Societies

If the eighteenth century marked the expansion of Baptist missionary endeavor in America, the nineteenth century took the expansion to the uttermost parts of the earth. While in the earlier century mission work was carried on through the associations, the new century would see the organization and growth of mission societies. However, these mission societies engaged only in foreign mission interests until a home mission society was formed in 1832. The associations, nevertheless, continued until mid-century with their programs of home mission endeavor. Gradually the associations became forums for missions—

collecting funds and informing the churches of the work of the agencies.

This new era had its beginning in 1792 when William Carey delivered a sermon to the Northampton Baptist Association in Nottingham, England, in which he implored his brethren to accept the responsibility of taking the gospel to the heathen. At that very meeting the association approved a motion that resulted in the formation of the Particular Baptist Society for the Propagation of the Gospel among the Heathen.

Some attention should be given to the fact that the organization of this society marked a different approach to cooperative Baptist work, which led to several controversies in the next century and a half. The society was formed in the back parlor of a private home in Kettering, England, by twelve ministers. It was neither a committee of the association nor of the churches, although it was, without question, the product of that Northampton association meeting.

Dr. Neely remarks:

The persistence and persuasive influence of Carey on his fellow ministers and messengers and their decision to form the new missionary society cannot be overdramatized, especially when one considers the paucity of their resources, the apparent apathy, the scornful attitude of virtually all the Baptist leaders in London towards the goings-on [in] that "obscure county association" and the subsequent impact of the decision at Kettering.[4]

Robert Baker contended that, in America, the organization of the mission societies displaced the association as the entrepreneur of the mission enterprise. He said, "Although the association had been conducting missionary work for almost half a century, within a decade the society plan was almost universally adopted in American Baptist life."[5]

The first Baptist missionary society in America was organized in 1802 by fourteen women in Boston. It is estimated that during the first decade of the nineteenth century, sixty-five missionary societies were formed north of Philadelphia, and some also in the South.

From Societies to Conventions

Contrary to the current presumption of many that associations grew into conventions, the facts are that conventions grew out of mission societies and were originally formed primarily for the purpose of promoting missions. David Benedict, recalling the missionary effort of the early 1800s, said, "A number of our oldest State Conventions grew out of the early societies for domestic missions."[6]

Perhaps the most important event to affect the modus operandi of missionary work was the organization of the Triennial Convention of 1814. The convention was called by agreement of the Baptist associations throughout the country. It met in the First Baptist Church of Philadelphia and the thirty-three persons presented Baptist associations. Half of the delegates were from the Philadelphia Association. The organization formed was called The General Missionary Convention of the Baptist Denomination in the United States of America for Foreign Missions. Significant portions of the constitution read as follows:

> We, the delegated from the Missionary Societies, and other religious bodies of the Baptist denomination . . . met in convention . . . for the purpose of carrying into effect the benevolent intentions of our constituents, by organizing a plan for eliciting, combining, and directing the energies of the whole denomination in one sacred effort. . . .[7]

The membership of this convention was "Delegates, not exceeding two in number from each of the several missionary societies, and other religious bodies of the Baptist denomination . . . which shall each regularly contribute to the general missionary fund, a sum amounting at least to one hundred dollars per annum."[8]

Since the convention met only once every three years, a board of commissioners was provided: ". . . twenty-one Commissioners, who shall be members of the said societies, churches or other religious bodies aforesaid. . . ."[9]

Of great importance is the difference in organization between the convention and the association. The convention consisted of *delegates* of mission societies and *religious bodies* rather than *messengers* from *churches*. The purpose of the convention was for "eliciting, combining and directing the energies of the whole denomination. . . ."[10] and membership in the convention was based on the contribution of at least one hundred dollars.

In 1844, because of tensions caused by slavery and the abolitionist movement, and because the acting board of the

General Foreign Mission Convention refused to appoint a slaveholder as a missionary, a call went out from the Virginia Baptist Foreign Mission Society for a convention to be held in May 1845 at Augusta, Georgia. It was here that the Southern Baptist Convention was formed. Robert Torbet describes it as "a new type of Baptist organization, being a firmly centralized denominational body functioning through various mission boards."[11] The charter of the Southern Baptist Convention contained language similar to that of the Triennial Convention. It stated:

> [A list of names] and others, either associates or successors, be and are hereby incorporated and made a body politic by the name and style of the Southern Baptist Convention . . . said corporation being created for the purpose of eliciting, combining and directing the energies of the Baptist denomination of Christians. . . .[12]

Differing elements in this new convention consisted in a system of boards that were an integral part of the convention. Of this system, Dr. J. B. Gambrell, former president of the SBC, said, "These general bodies occupy a sphere of their own entirely outside the limits of the churches."[13] Messengers are apportioned from the churches on the basis of $250 contribution or 250 members per messenger.

In the North, the society method of missions continued until 1907 through the American Baptist Missionary Union. The Northern Baptist Convention came into existence that year, born of the emphasis on more efficient organization so characteristic of big business at the turn of the century, and the desire of theological liberals like Shailer Mathews, of the University of Chicago, to form an organization to convert society by the Social Gospel. The Northern Baptist Convention, like the Triennial and Southern Conventions, was organized in the interest of missions. By 1950 Baptist historian Torbet wrote:

> The changes which have marked the past fifty years have been concerned with a shift of organizational emphasis from the local church and association to state and national agencies. This trend has been particularly prevalent among Northern Baptists.[14]

Other Mission Systems among Baptists
Direct Gospel Missions

Those who use the direct system reject organization in

mission endeavors and maintain that all money be sent directly to the missionary. It is their contention that all church enterprises, such as schools and orphanages, be owned and controlled by individual churches.

Independent Board System

Independent Baptist boards are autonomous and not an organizational part of any association or convention. In the case of the GARBC, those missions desiring such recognition are "approved" annually by the Council of Eighteen, who are elected by the messengers from the churches.

The mission agencies are self-perpetuating, and the approval of missionaries, their support and the conduct of their work is under the direction of the agency. The missions require that the missionary appointee be commissioned by the local church for missionary service. The missionary is ultimately answerable to the local church, but the direct supervision is effected by the mission. The mission agencies are usually cooperative and sympathetic to the concerns of a local church. When a serious problem exists or disciplinary action must be taken, it is customary for the mission to act in close cooperation with the commissioning church. There may, of course, be an occasional breakdown in communication in such cases.

The Associational System

This system is older than the society or convention systems. It is used today by the Baptist Missionary Association. The Missionary Committee is composed of twenty-five workers selected at the annual meeting and one chosen by each local church in the fellowship. The Missionary Committee thus has direct church authority in all its deliberations. The missionary must give evidence that he is called of God, endorsed and commissioned by his local church. The churches, through their messengers (three from each church) choose the missionaries who are to serve all of them. According to this plan, the churches have a direct voice in missions.[15]

Antimission Controversies

There were two significant antimission controversies in America. The first followed the organization of the Triennial Convention in 1814. Many Baptists viewed the Triennial

Convention with grave misgivings, seeing its establishment and its board of commissioners as a trend toward irreversible centralization and the usurpation of authority reserved for the local church. There were also some who felt that the foreign missions effort was an interference with the sovereignty of God.

The controversy raged from 1820 to 1840. Not only did many churches align themselves with this movement, but entire associations defected. This controversy divided the Baptists in America into two camps.

The second antimission controversy arose after the organization of the Southern Baptist Convention. The "gospel mission" controversy, as it was called, was led by two prominent men, J. R. Graves and J. M. Pendleton. These men and their followers taught what is called "Old Landmarkism," which was based on the desire to restore the purity of the early church by keeping a faithful Baptist membership and ministry.

The Landmarkers protested against the financial basis of representation in the convention and the supervision of missions by convention boards. J. R. Graves wrote in the *Tennessee Baptist* in 1860:

The first radical fault in our missionary scheme is that it is a centralization—a centralized operation. It takes out of the hands of many of the churches and places our missionary operations in the hands of a few. Such has been the character of our missionary organizations, and they have failed; the present is a failure; all the future ones of a similar kind will be. The churches are called upon to surrender all intimate concern in the management of and planning for, and directing the missionaries and the mission work into the hands of a central board; and content themselves with supplying the funds called upon by agents.[16]

The Landmark movement had a significant impact on the Southern Baptist Convention and eventually resulted in the organization of the General Association of Baptist Churches in 1902 (not to be confused with the General Association of Regular Baptist Churches, 1932) by the withdrawal of fifty-two churches in the Southwest from the Southern Baptist Convention.

End Notes

[1] Alan Neely, "A History of Associational Involvement in

Missions," *Baptist History and Heritage,* vol. 17, no. 2 (Nashville: Southern Baptist Historical Society, 1982), p. 22. [These materials originally appeared in the April, 1982, issue of *Baptist History and Heritage,* publication of the Historical Commission of the Southern Baptist Convention. Used by permission.]

[2] Henry C. Vedder, "Baptists of the Middle States," *A Century of Baptist Achievements,* ed. A. H. Newman (Philadelphia: American Baptist Publication Society, 1901), p. 73.

[3] Morgan Edwards, "Materials toward a History of Baptists in the Providence of North Carolina (1772)," *North Carolina Historical Review,* ed. G. W. Paschel (January–October, 1930), n.p.

[4] Neely, p. 22.

[5] Robert A. Baker, *The Southern Baptist Convention and Its People* (Nashville: Broadman Press, 1974), pp. 98, 100.

[6] Benedict, *Fifty Years,* p. 24.

[7] Porter Routh, *77,000 Churches* (Nashville: Broadman Press, 1964), pp. 16, 17.

[8] Ibid.

[9] Ibid.

[10] Ibid.

[11] Robert G. Torbet, *A History of Baptists* (Valley Forge, PA: Judson Press, 1969), p. 293.

[12] Jackson, *Doctrine and History,* p. 91.

[13] Ibid.

[14] Torbet, p. 293.

[15] Jackson, p. 97.

[16] Ibid., p. 93.

CONCLUDING THOUGHTS

The preceding chapters in this book have been concerned primarily with the first century of Baptist associations in America. That period may be dated from the organization of the Philadelphia Baptist Association in 1707 to the Triennial Convention in 1814, or, roughly, the eighteenth century.

The organization of the Triennial Convention marked a new era among Baptists in America: an era of great growth, of missionary endeavor and of increasing organization in the Baptist denomination. The nineteenth century also brought the scourge of liberalism, or "modernism," as it was called. This religious rationalism invaded the ranks of Baptists and gave rise to a third period in American Baptist history, the twentieth-century struggle for orthodoxy.

About the year 1875, the Bible conference movement was started in order to counteract the influence of modernism in the schools and denominations. This movement was augmented by the establishing of Bible institutes and eventually led to a battle for the denominations. The Baptists, particularly in the North, were at the vanguard of this battle. The term "fundamentalist" was first used in connection with the battle for the Northern Baptist Convention. Since the mid-1920s, there has been a realignment of fundamental Baptists in associations of churches, fellowships of individuals and "independents" who decline to enter into formal church relations.

Many Baptist churches over the past fifty years have entered into cooperation with other denominations in order to support sound missionary, educational or social projects through interdenominational agencies. A new denomination has thus arisen, the "interdenominational denomination," which bases its cooperative work on the concept of the universal or "invisible" church rather than the local church. As a result of this type of cooperation, many Baptist churches have lost their distinctiveness and are no longer distinctively Baptist in doctrine and polity. Some Baptist churches are calling pastors who are not able to identify the Baptist distinctives.

Many pastors and churches shy away from association because they fear an intrusion upon their independence. It is my belief that this fear is caused by a misunderstanding of the nature of an association, and especially of the distinction between an association and a convention. The fear is compounded by stories of convention excesses. Here I would stress again that there are great differences between a convention and an association.

Having enjoyed the blessings and benefits of association for all of my ministry, I am much in favor of this type of relationship among Baptist churches. Because there are many shades of thought among Baptists, it is of value to associate with those who share our doctrinal and philosophical emphases. Some Baptists lay emphasis on their Calvinism or non-Calvinism. Some are premillennial; others, amillennial. Some are separatist and some are inclusive in their relationships. By gathering in associations, we can preserve these emphases while at the same time preserving our Baptist distinctives.

Associations conserve the emphasis on congregational polity because relationship is determined by congregational vote, and the association is composed of messengers chosen by the local church.

In these closing years of the twentieth century, it is increasingly important that fellowships of churches stand together to preserve religious liberty in a nation that is becoming increasingly indifferent and even hostile to Biblical Christianity. In the eighteenth century, Baptists struggled to preserve their identity and their religious liberty. Today we are faced with a similar problem. Colonial Baptists did not join in mutual endeavors with other denominations. And they never sat at the communion table with them because to do so would be a denial of all that they believed about baptism and the nature of the church.

Many years of interdenominational cooperation have blinded the eyes of some Baptists to the nature of our beliefs. Our distinctives are distinctives on the doctrine of the *church!* And, like Baptists of other ages, we believe these truths because they are taught in the Word of God.

ESSAY ON THE POWER AND DUTY OF AN ASSOCIATION

by Benjamin Griffith

That an Association is not a superior judicature, having such superior power over the churches concerned; but that each particular church hath a complete power and authority from Jesus Christ, to administer to all gospel ordinances, provided they have a sufficiency of officers duly qualified, or that they be supplied by the officers of another sister church or churches, as baptism, and the Lord's Supper, &c.; and to receive in and cast out, and also to try and ordain their own officers, and to exercise every part of gospel discipline and church government, independent of any other church or assembly whatever.

And that several such independent churches, where Providence gives them their situation convenient, may, and ought, for their mutual strength, counsel, and other valuable advantages, by their voluntary and free consent, to enter into an agreement and confederation, as is hinted in our printed Narrative of discipline, pages 59, 60, 61.

Such churches there must be agreeing in doctrine and practice, and independent in their authority and church power, before they can enter into a confederation, as aforesaid, and choose delegates or representative, or associate together; and thus the several independent churches being the constituents, the association, council or assembly of their delegates, when assembled, is not to be deemed a superior judicature, as having a superintendency over the churches, but subservient to the churches, in what may concern all the churches in general, or any one church in particular; and, though no power can regularly arise above its fountain from where it rises, yet we are of opinion, that an Association of the delegates of associate churches have a very considerable power in their hands, respecting those churches in their confederation; for if the agreement of several distinct churches, in sound doctrine and regular practice, be the first motive, ground, and foundation or basis of their confederation, then it must naturally follow, that a defection in doctrine or practice in any church, in such confederation, or any party in any such church, is ground sufficient for an Association to withdraw from such a church or party so deviating or making deflection, and to exclude such from them in some formal manner, and to advertise all the churches in confederation thereof, in order that every church in confederation may withdraw from such in all acts of church communion, to the end they may be ashamed, and that all the churches may discountenance such, and bear testimony against the defection.

Such withdrawing from a defective or disorderly church, or that ought to be towards a delinquent church, is such as ariseth from their voluntary confederation aforesaid, and not only from the general duty that is incumbent on all orthodox persons, and churches to do, where no such confederation is entered into, as 2 Cor. vi. 16, 17. Now, from that general duty to withdraw from defective persons or churches, there can no more be done, than to desist from such acts of fellowship as subsisted before the withdrawing, which is merely negative, and in no wise any thing positive. Churches, as they are pillars of truth, may, and ought to endeavor to promote truth among others also; which endeavors, if they prove fruitless, as they are but mystico modo, they may be withdrawn; the withdrawing, therefore, must be accordingly; which is only to cease from future endeavors, leaving the objects as they were or are. But if there be a confederation and incorporation, by mutual and voluntary consent, as the Association of churches must and ought to be, then something positive may and ought to be done; and, though an Association ought not to assume a power to excommunicate or deliver a defective or disorderly church to Satan, as some do claim, yet it is a power sufficient to exclude the delegates of a defective or disorderly church from an Association, and to refuse their presence at their consultations, and to advise all the churches in confederation to do so too. A godly man may, and ought to withdraw, not only from a heathen, but from such as have the form of godliness, if they appear to want the power of it, 2 Tim. iii. 5, by the same parity of reason the saints, in what capacity soever they may be considered, may withdraw from defective or disorderly churches or persons; but excommunicate they cannot, there being no institution to authorize them to do so. But in the capacity of a congregational church, dealing with her own members, an Association, then, of the delegates of associate churches, may exclude and withdraw from defective and unsound or disorderly churches or persons, in manner abovesaid; and this will appear regular and justifiable by the light and law of nature, as is apparent in the conduct and practice of all regular civil and political corporations and confederations whatsoever; who all of them have certain rules to exclude delinquents from the societies, as well as for others to accede thereunto.

We judge those things in the 15th chapter of the Acts of the Apostles to be imitable by an Association, viz.: 1st, their disowning of the erroneous and judaising teachers, saying, to whom we gave no such commandment, verse 24; 2ndly, the sending to delegated persons of their own number, with Paul and Barnabas, to support their sentence in the place where the debate sprung up, verse 25; and a third thing followed in consequence thereof, viz., a delivering of the decrees to the other churches, to be observed, as well as the church of Antioch, chap. xvi. 4. Consistent therewith, the practice of after ages is found to be; when, because they had no council, synod, or association to convene, of course they called a council, in order to make head against any error or disorders, when in any particular church, such things grew too big for a particular church peaceable to determine, as the case about circumcision was at Antioch. In such cases all the churches were looked upon as one church, and all the bishops as universal, because of the unity of the faith and conformity of practice which ought to be in the churches of Christ; though in all other cases, the several distinct churches acted independent of each other, as Cyprian relates the practice of his time, viz.: That the bishops were so united in one body, that if any one of the body broached any heresy, or began to waste and tear the flock of Christ, all the rest came immediately to its rescue. Cyprian, cited by Bingham, book 2, page 101. And the same author observes, that they disowned the faulty, and advertised all the church of the same. And Mr. Crosby relates, that an Association in London did disown a certain disorderly church in London, and did caution all the churches they were related to, not to countenance them in any way, nor to suffer their members to frequent their meetings; and thus an Association may disown and withdraw from a defective or disorderly church, and advise the churches related to them to withdraw from, and to discountenance such as aforesaid, without exceeding the bounds of their power.

And further, that an Association of the delegates of confederate churches may doctrinally declare any person or party in a church, who are defective in principles or disorderly in practice, to be censurable, when the affair comes under their cognizance, and without exceeding the bounds of their power and duty, to advise the church that such belong unto, how to deal with such, according to the rule of gospel discipline; and also to strengthen such a church, and assist her, if need be, by sending able men of their own number to help the church in executing the power vested in her by the ordinance of Jesus Christ, and to stand by her, and to defend her against the insults of such offending persons or parties.

The above is a transcript of the said essay, according to the order given by the said Association, which was ordered to be taken without the then introduction and singularity. Taking the substance and contents thereof as the judgment of the Association, respecting their power and duty.

Consented to and transcribed by me, Benjamin Griffith. Signed by the whole Association.

Philadelphia, September 19, 1749

From the *Minutes of the Philadelphia Baptist Association, 1707–1807.* A. D. Gillette, ed. (Minneapolis: James Publishing Co., n.d.), pp. 60–63.

OLDEST BAPTIST ASSOCIATIONS IN AMERICA

1. Philadelphia Association, 1707
2. Charleston Association, South Carolina, 1751
3. Sandy Creek Association, North Carolina, 1758
4. Kehukee Association, North Carolina, 1765
5. Ketocton Association, Virginia, 1766
6. Warren Association, Rhode Island, 1767
7. Stonington Association, Connecticut, 1772
8. Redstone Association, Pennsylvania, 1776
9. New Hampshire Association, 1776
10. Shaftsbury Association, Vermont, 1781
11. Woodstock Association, Vermont, 1783
12. Georgia Association, 1784
13. Holston Association, Tennessee, 1786
14. Bowdoinham Association, Maine, 1787
15. Vermont Association, 1787

ON CHURCH DISCIPLINE IN 1826

Among my own papers, I find one "On Church Discipline," dates [sic] 1826. It appears to be the rough draft of an essay which was read before a Ministers' Meeting. Among the greatest defects of our churches at that time, according to the document under consideration, were,

1. The want of more strictness in the duties of personal and family religion, and of pious instruction to children and domestics;

2. Of more faithfulness in following the directions of the 18th of Matthew, relative to private offenses, whereby an abundance of extra trouble came upon the churches;

3. Of plain dealing with erring church members;

4. Of procrastination and hurtful delays in instituting church dealings with such members, under the false plea of patience and charity;

5. Of more frequent, friendly, old-fashioned, Christian intercourse, and familiarity with each other, in consequence of which coldness and distance ensue;

6. Of liberality in contributing to the support of the gospel at home and abroad;

7. Of giving more explicit instructions to new members at first, and of enforcing obedience to them afterwards.

Such were my views of the state of church discipline among the Baptists one third of a century since; and it is to be feared they have not made much improvement in the business since.

—*Fifty Years Among the Baptists*
by David Benedict
published in 1860

Warrant for Arrest of Elders Saunders and McClannahan

Culpeper, Sct.:

Whereas we have received information that Nathaniel Saunders and William McClannahan, stiling themselves Protestant dissenters, does teach and preach contrary to the laws and usages of the Kingdom of Great Britain, raising sedition and stirring up strife amongst His Majestie's leige people.

Therefore in His Majestie's name we require you, Samuel Ferguson and John Lillard, to take Nathaniel Saunders and William McClannahan and their abettors and bring before some justice of the peace for the said county to be examined touching the charge, and we do hereby command all His Majestie's subjects to be aiding and assisting in the due execution thereof.

Given under our hands this 21st day of August, 1773.

John Slaughter,

George Wetherall.

To the Sheriff or any Constable of this county, or to Samuel Ferguson and John Lillard.

Executed: Pr Samuel Ferguson,

John Lillard.

Printed in Robert B. Semple, *History of the Baptists in Virginia* (Lafayette, TN: Church History Research and Archives, 1976), p. 481.

LETTER WRITTEN IN MIDDLESEX JAIL BY ELDER JOHN WALLER

Urbanna Prison, Middlesex County, August 12, 1771.

Dear Brother in the Lord;

At a meeting which was held at Brother McCan's, in this county, last Saturday, while Brother William Webber was addressing the congregation from James ii., 18, there came running toward him, in a most furious rage, Captain James Montague, a magistrate of the county, followed by the parson of the parish and several others, who seemed greatly exasperated. The magistrate and another took hold of Brother Webber, and dragging him from the stage, delivered him, with Brethren Wafford, Robert Ware, Richard Faulkner, James Greenwood and myself, into custody, and commanded that we should be brought before him for trial. Brother Wafford was severely scourged, and Brother Henry Street received one lash from one of the persecutors, who was prevented from proceeding to further violence by his companions. To be short, I may inform you that we were carried before the above-mentioned magistrate, who, with the parson and some others, carried us one by one into a room and examined our pockets and wallets for firearms, &c., charging us with carrying on a meeting against the authority of the land. Finding none, we were asked if we had license to preach in the county; and learning we had not, it was required of us to give bond and security not to preach any more in this county, which we modestly refused to do; whereupon, after dismissing Brother Wafford, with a charge to make his escape out of the county by twelve o'clock the next day on pain of imprisonment, and dismissing Brother Faulkner, the rest of us were delivered to the sheriff and sent to close jail, with a charge not to let us walk in the air until courtday. Blessed by God, the sheriff and jailer have treated us with as much kindness as could have been expected from strangers. May the Lord reward them for it! Yesterday we had a large number of people to hear us preach; and among others, many of the great ones of the land; who behaved well while one of us discoursed on the new birth. We find the Lord gracious and kind to us beyond expression in our afflictions. We cannot tell how long we shall be kept in bonds; we therefore beseech, dear brother, that you and the church supplicate night and day for us, our benefactors and our persecutors.

I have to inform you that six of our brethren are confined in Caroline jail, viz., Brethren Lewis Craig, John and Bartholomew Choning. The most dreadful threatenings are raised in the neighboring counties against the Lord's faithful and humble followers.

Excuse haste. Adieu.

John Waller.

From Robert B. Semple, *History of the Baptists in Virginia*, pp. 481–483.

Memorial for Lewis Craig, John Waller, Jr., and James Chiles, who were imprisoned for preaching

TO THE GENERAL COMMITTEE REPRESENTING THE UNITED BAPTIST CHURCHES IN VIRGINIA

Gentlemen,

I request that you will accept my best acknowledgements for your congratulation on my appointment to the first office in the nation. The kind manner in which you mention my past conduct equally claims the expression of my gratitude. After we had, by the smiles of Divine Providence on our exertions, obtained the object for which we contended, I retired at the conclusion of the war with the idea that my country could have no farther occasion for my services, and with the intention of never entering again into public life; but when the exigencies of my country seemed to require me once more to engage in public affairs, an honest conviction of duty superseded my former resolution and became my apology for deviating from the happy plan which I had adopted.

If I could have entertained the slightest apprehension that the Constitution framed in the convention where I had the honor to preside might possibly endanger the religious rights of any ecclesiastical society, certainly I would never have placed my signature to it; and if I could now conceive that the General Government might ever be so administered as to render the liberty of conscience insecure, I beg you will be persuaded that no one would be more zealous than myself to establish effectual barriers against the horrors of spiritual tyranny and every species of religious persecution.

For you doubtless remember I have often expressed my sentiments that every man conducting himself as a good citizen, and being accountable to God alone for his religious opinions, ought to be protected in worshipping the Deity according to the dictates of his own conscience.

While I recollect with satisfaction that the religious society of which you are members have been throughout America, uniformly and almost unanimously, the firm friends to civil liberty, and the persevering promoters of our glorious revolution, I cannot hesitate to believe that they will be faithful supporters of a free yet efficient General Government. Under this pleasing expectation I rejoice to assure them that they may rely upon my best wishes and endeavors to advance their prosperity.

In the meantime be assured, gentlemen, that I entertain a proper sense of your fervent supplication to God for my temporal and eternal happiness.

I am, gentlemen, your most obedient servant,
George Washington.

From Robert B. Semple, *History of the Baptists in Virginia*, pp. 487–489.

Letter to the Buck Mountain Baptist Church

Several congratulatory addresses were sent to Mr. Jefferson on his retirement from the presidency by different Baptist bodies in Virginia. The spirit of his replies is well expressed in the following letter to the Buck Mountain Baptist Church:

Monticello, April 13, 1809.

I thank you, my friends and neighbors, for your kind congratulations on my return to my native home, and of the opportunities it will give me of enjoying, amidst your affections, the comforts of retirement and rest. Your approbation of my conduct is the more valued as you have best known me, and is an ample reward for any services I may have rendered. We have acted together from the origin to the end of a memorable Revolution, and we have contributed each in the line allotted to us our endeavors to render its issues a permanent blessing to our country. That our social intercourse may, to the evening of our days, be cheered and cemented by witnessing the freedom and happiness for which we have labored, will be my constant prayer.

Accept the offering of my affectionate esteem and respect. Thomas Jefferson.

From Robert B. Semple, *History of the Baptists in Virginia,* pp. 509–510.

ORIGINAL MINUTES OF THE BAPTIST MISSIONARY SOCIETY

At a Ministers Meeting at Kettering the following Resolutions were agreed to Oct. 2. 1792.

I. Desirous of making an effort for the propagation of the gospel amongst the heathens, agreeable to what is intimated in Mr. Carey's late publication on that subject, we whose names are annexed to the subsequent subscriptions, do solemnly agree to act in Society together for that purpose.

II. As in the present divided state of Christendom it seems that each denomination by exerting itself separately is most likely to accomplish the great ends of a mission, it is agreed that this Society be called *The Particular Baptist Society, for propagating the gospel amongst the heathen.*

III. As such an undertaking must need be attended with expense, we agree immediately to open a subscription for that purpose, and to recommend it to others.

N.B. The names of the subscribers and amount of the subscriptions were as follows,

Rev. John Ryland	—2..2..0
Reynold Hogg	—2..2..0
John Sutcliff	—1..1..0
Andrew Fuller	—1..1..0
Abraham Greenwood	—1..1..0
Edward Sharman	—1..1..0
Samuel Pearce	—1..1..0
Mr. Joseph Timms	—1..1..0
	10..10..0

bro't forward	—10..10..0
Rev. William Heighton	—10..6
William Staughton	—10..6
Joshua Burton	—10..6
Thomas Blundel	—10..6
John Eayre	<u>—10..6</u>
	13:2:6

IV. Every person who shall subscribe 10, or 10/6 annually, shall be considered as a member.

V. That Messrs. John Ryland, John Sutcliff, William Carey, Reynold Hagg, and Andrew Fuller be appointed a committee, three of whom shall be empowered to act.

VI. That Rev. Reynold Hagg be appointed Treasurer, and Rev. Andrew Fuller Secretary.

VII. That the subscriptions be paid in at the Northampton Ministers meeting to be held Oct. 31st at which time the subject shall be considered more particularly.

MONUMENT MARKING MADISON-LELAND MEETING

This monument, located on State Route 20 (the Constitution Route) about seven miles east of Orange, marks a possible site of the meeting between James Madison and John Leland.

Madison was a candidate for delegate to the Convention called to decide whether Virginia should ratify the proposed Federal Constitution. Leland was an influential Baptist preacher.

According to tradition, Madison persuaded Leland, and hence the Orange Baptists, to support his candidacy in favor of ratification. In turn, he assured the Baptist preacher that he would do all in his power to see that civil rights, including religious freedom, would be incorporated into the Constitution by amendment.

NOTES

Notes

NOTES